# Becoming Super Parents: a Guide to Great Parenting

Sundvall Alan William

Published by Sundvall Alan William, 2024.

While every precaution has been taken in the preparation of this book, the publisher assumes no responsibility for errors or omissions, or for damages resulting from the use of the information contained herein.

BECOMING SUPER PARENTS: A GUIDE TO GREAT PARENTING

**First edition. April 2, 2024.**



ISBN: 979-8224664337

Written by Sundvall Alan William.

# Table of Contents

# Chapter 1: Introduction

## - Defining Great Parenting

Great parenting can be defined as the intentional and consistent effort to nurture, support, and guide children in their physical, emotional, social, and cognitive development. It involves creating a loving and nurturing environment where children feel safe, supported, and encouraged to explore, learn, and grow. Great parents are emotionally available and responsive to their children's needs, providing both love and discipline in appropriate measures. They set clear boundaries and expectations while also fostering independence and autonomy in their children.

One key aspect of great parenting is the ability to prioritize the well-being and development of the child above all else. This means that parents make decisions and choices that are in the best interest of their children, even if it may not always be easy or convenient for them. Great parents understand that raising children is a long-term commitment that requires patience, sacrifice, and dedication.

Effective communication is another hallmark of great parenting. Parents who communicate openly and honestly with their children establish a foundation of trust and mutual respect. They listen actively to their children's thoughts, feelings, and concerns, and validate their experiences. By fostering open communication, parents create a supportive and nurturing environment where children feel safe expressing themselves and seeking guidance.

Additionally, great parents are actively involved in their children's lives, taking an interest in their activities, hobbies, and friendships. They attend school events, extracurricular activities, and parent-teacher conferences, showing their children that they value and support their interests and accomplishments. This involvement helps parents stay connected to their children's lives and provides opportunities to offer guidance and support when needed.

Discipline is also an important aspect of great parenting. While discipline is often associated with punishment, great parents understand that effective discipline is about teaching and guiding children towards responsible behavior and positive decision-making. They set clear and consistent rules and expectations, and enforce consequences when needed, but do so in a loving and respectful manner. Great parents use discipline as a tool for teaching children valuable life skills such as responsibility, self-control, and empathy.

All in all, great parents prioritize self-care and personal growth. Parenting can be stressful and demanding, and it is important for parents to take care of themselves both physically and emotionally in order to be the best parents they can be. This may involve seeking support from friends, family, or professionals, engaging in self-care activities, or pursuing personal interests and passions. By taking care of themselves, parents are better able to show up as their best selves for their children and model healthy behaviors and coping strategies. It involves creating a nurturing and supportive environment, prioritizing the well-being and development of the child, fostering open communication, being actively involved in their children's lives, using effective discipline strategies, and prioritizing self-care and personal growth. While no parent is perfect, striving towards these ideals can help create a positive and loving relationship between parents and children that lasts a lifetime.

## - Importance of Parenting

Parenting is a crucial aspect of raising children and plays a significant role in their development and well-being. Parents are not only responsible for providing their children with basic necessities such as food, shelter, and clothing, but they also have a profound impact on their emotional, social, and cognitive development. Research has shown that the quality of parenting a child receives can have long-lasting effects on their future outcomes, including academic achievement, career success, and mental health. Therefore, it is essential for parents to be aware of the importance of their role in shaping their children's lives and to strive to be the best caregivers they can be.

One of the key aspects of parenting is the establishment of a secure attachment between parent and child. Attachment theory, developed by psychologist John Bowlby, posits that a strong emotional bond between a child and their caregiver is essential for their healthy development. Children who have a secure attachment to their parents are more likely to have positive self-esteem, develop healthy relationships with others, and exhibit better emotional regulation. On the other hand, children who experience insecure attachments may struggle with feelings of anxiety, low self-worth, and difficulty forming close relationships.

In addition to fostering a secure attachment, parents also play a crucial role in setting boundaries and providing structure for their children. Consistent discipline and clear expectations help children learn self-control and develop a sense of responsibility. Without appropriate boundaries, children may struggle with impulsive behavior, defiance, and difficulty following rules. By establishing rules and consequences for their actions, parents can help their children learn the importance of accountability and make responsible decisions.

Furthermore, the quality of communication between parents and children is essential for healthy development. Open and honest communication helps children develop language skills, express their emotions, and build strong relationships with others. Parents who engage in meaningful conversations with their children create a safe space for them to share their thoughts and feelings, fostering a sense of trust and connection. Additionally, effective communication allows parents to teach their children important life skills, such as problem-solving, conflict resolution, and emotional intelligence.

Parenting also involves providing children with guidance and support as they navigate the challenges of growing up. As children develop and mature, they encounter various obstacles and uncertainties that can be overwhelming. Parents who offer unconditional love, encouragement, and guidance help their children build resilience and cope with adversity. By being present and attentive, parents can help their children develop a sense of security and confidence in themselves, enabling them to thrive and succeed in all areas of their lives. The importance of parenting cannot be overstated, as the quality of care and guidance that children receive from their parents has a lasting impact on their development and well-being. By fostering secure attachments, setting boundaries, communicating effectively, and providing guidance and support, parents can help their children grow into happy, healthy, and successful individuals. It is essential for parents to understand the significance of their role in shaping their children's lives and to strive to be positive and nurturing caregivers. Through thoughtful and intentional parenting practices, parents can create a supportive and loving environment that sets their children up for success in all aspects of their lives.

# Chapter 2: Understanding Child Development

## - Stages of Child Development

Child development is a complex and fascinating process that encompasses various stages, each with its own unique characteristics and milestones. Understanding these stages is crucial for parents, educators, and healthcare professionals in order to provide appropriate support and guidance to children as they grow and mature. In this discussion, we will explore the different stages of child development and highlight key aspects of each stage.

The first stage of child development is the prenatal period, which begins at conception and lasts until birth. During this stage, the fetus undergoes rapid growth and development, with major organs and systems forming and maturing. Prenatal care is essential during this stage to ensure the health and well-being of both the mother and the developing baby. Factors such as nutrition, maternal health, and environmental influences can have a significant impact on fetal development. Prenatal screening and monitoring are important tools for assessing the health and progress of the fetus and identifying any potential issues that may require intervention.

The next stage of child development is infancy, which typically spans from birth to around 2 years of age. Infants experience dramatic physical, cognitive, and social development during this stage, as they learn to interact with their environment and form attachments with caregivers. Motor skills, language development, and social responsiveness are key areas of growth during infancy. Newborns exhibit reflexive behaviors such as sucking and rooting, while older infants are able to sit up, crawl, and eventually walk. Language development progresses from cooing and babbling to producing words and simple sentences. Social development in infancy is characterized by the formation of bonds with caregivers and the beginning of social interactions with others.

The toddler stage follows infancy and typically lasts from around 2 to 3 years of age. Toddlers are characterized by their exploration and experimentation with their environment, as they begin to walk, talk, and assert their independence. This stage is marked by rapid cognitive and social development, as toddlers learn to problem-solve, communicate, and interact with others. Language development continues to progress, with toddlers acquiring a larger vocabulary and starting to use more complex sentence structures. Socially, toddlers start to engage in play with peers and show increased awareness of others' emotions and intentions. The emergence of temper tantrums and defiant behaviors is common during this stage as toddlers test boundaries and assert their autonomy.

The preschool stage spans from around 3 to 5 years of age and is characterized by significant advances in language, cognitive, and social development. Preschoolers are curious and eager learners, as they explore their world and acquire new skills and knowledge. Language development continues to progress, with preschoolers becoming more adept at expressing themselves verbally and engaging in conversations. Cognitive development advances as preschoolers develop problem-solving skills, spatial awareness, and a basic understanding of numbers and letters. Socially, preschoolers engage in more complex play and begin to form friendships with peers. They also start to develop a sense of empathy and learn to cooperate and take turns in social interactions.

The school-age stage follows preschool and typically spans from around 6 to 12 years of age. School-age children experience significant physical, cognitive, and social development as they navigate the challenges of formal education and peer relationships. Physical development during this stage is characterized by growth spurts and changes in body composition. Cognitive development advances as children acquire more advanced problem-solving skills, critical thinking abilities, and academic knowledge. Socially, school-age children form strong peer relationships and develop a sense of identity and self-esteem. They also begin to demonstrate empathy, cooperation, and a sense of fairness in their interactions with others.

The adolescent stage follows the school-age stage and spans from around 13 to 18 years of age. Adolescents undergo significant physical, cognitive, and social development as they transition from childhood to adulthood. Physical development is marked by puberty, which involves physical changes such as growth spurts, sexual maturation, and changes in body composition. Cognitive development advances as adolescents develop more abstract thinking skills, self-awareness, and a sense of identity. Socially, adolescents experience increased autonomy and independence from their parents, as they form peer relationships, explore their interests and values, and begin to establish their own identity. Understanding these stages is essential for parents, educators, and healthcare professionals to support children's growth and development effectively. By recognizing and nurturing the physical, cognitive, and social aspects of child development at each stage, we can help children reach their full potential and thrive in their journey toward adulthood.

# - Factors influencing Child Development

Child development is a complex and multifaceted process that is influenced by a wide range of factors. These factors can be broadly categorized into two main groups: nature and nurture. Nature refers to the genetic and biological factors that a child inherits from their parents, while nurture refers to the environmental influences and experiences that shape a child's development.

One of the primary factors influencing child development is genetics. Each child is born with a unique set of genetic predispositions that contribute to their physical, cognitive, emotional, and social development. For example, genes play a significant role in determining a child's height, eye color, and susceptibility to certain illnesses. Genetic factors also play a key role in shaping a child's temperament and personality traits. Studies have shown that genetic factors can influence a wide range of developmental outcomes, such as intelligence, aggression, and emotional stability.

In addition to genetics, environmental factors also play a critical role in shaping a child's development. The environment in which a child grows up can have a profound impact on their physical, cognitive, emotional, and social development. Environmental factors encompass a wide range of influences, including the child's home environment, family dynamics, socioeconomic status, cultural background, and access to educational opportunities. Research has shown that children who grow up in stable, nurturing environments tend to have better developmental outcomes than those who grow up in chaotic or stressful environments.

Parenting style is another important factor that influences child development. The way in which parents interact with their children can have a significant impact on their cognitive, emotional, and social development. For example, research has shown that children who are raised in authoritative parenting environments where parents are warm, responsive, and provide clear guidelines tend to have better developmental outcomes than children who are raised in authoritarian or permissive parenting environments. Authoritative parenting is characterized by high levels of warmth and responsiveness, combined with clear and consistent discipline.

The quality of early childhood education and care also plays a key role in shaping a child's development. High-quality early childhood education programs can provide children with a strong foundation for learning and social development. Research has shown that children who attend high-quality early childhood education programs tend to have better cognitive, language, and social skills than children who do not have access to such programs. Early childhood education programs that focus on promoting social-emotional development, language development, and early literacy skills are particularly beneficial for children's overall development.

Socioeconomic status is another important factor that influences child development. Children who grow up in poverty or low-income households are at increased risk for developmental delays and academic difficulties. Socioeconomic status influences a wide range of developmental outcomes, including cognitive development, language development, and academic achievement. Children from low-income backgrounds are more likely to experience chronic stress, malnutrition, and exposure to environmental toxins, all of which can have a negative impact on their development. In addition, children from low-income backgrounds are less likely to have access to high-quality educational opportunities, healthcare, and other resources that can support their development.

Cultural factors also play a significant role in shaping child development. Each culture has its own beliefs, values, and customs that influence how children are raised and socialized. Cultural factors can influence a wide range of developmental outcomes, including language development, social relationships, and emotional regulation. For example, some cultures place a high value on independence and assertiveness, while others prioritize cooperative and harmonious relationships. Cultural factors can also influence parenting practices, educational philosophies, and attitudes towards child-rearing. Genetics, environment, parenting style, early childhood education, socioeconomic status, and cultural factors all play a role in shaping a child's development. Understanding the various factors that influence child development can help parents, educators, and policymakers create supportive environments that promote positive developmental outcomes for all children. By recognizing the importance of both nature and nurture in shaping child development, we can work towards ensuring that every child has the opportunity to reach their full potential.

# - Importance of Understanding Child Development

Understanding child development is essential for anyone who works with children, whether it be educators, parents, caregivers, or healthcare professionals. Child development refers to the changes that occur in children as they grow and develop physically, emotionally, socially, and cognitively. By understanding child development, we are better equipped to support children in reaching their full potential and thriving in all areas of their lives.

One of the key reasons why understanding child development is important is that it provides a framework for identifying and addressing developmental delays or challenges. By being knowledgeable about typical developmental milestones, we can recognize when a child may be lagging behind in a certain area and provide appropriate interventions or support to help them catch up.

For example, if a child is having trouble with language development, understanding typical language milestones can help us identify when to seek assistance from a speech therapist.

Additionally, understanding child development allows us to create age-appropriate learning experiences and activities for children. Each stage of development brings with it unique abilities, interests, and challenges, and by tailoring our approach to the specific needs of each age group, we can maximize children's learning and growth. For example, young children who are in the sensorimotor stage of development benefit from hands-on, sensory-rich activities that engage their senses and promote exploration, whereas older children in the concrete operational stage may benefit from more structured and abstract learning tasks.

Furthermore, understanding child development helps us to foster positive social and emotional development in children. Children's social and emotional skills are crucial for building relationships, managing emotions, and navigating social situations. By understanding the typical progression of social and emotional development, we can support children in developing these skills at an appropriate pace and in a supportive environment. For example, understanding that preschool-aged children are just beginning to learn how to take turns and share can help us structure play activities that promote these skills.

In addition to supporting children's development, understanding child development is also important for promoting positive parenting practices. When parents have a solid understanding of their child's developmental needs and abilities, they are better equipped to respond to their child in a sensitive and supportive manner. For example, understanding that toddlers have limited impulse control can help parents set appropriate limits and provide guidance in a way that is developmentally appropriate. By understanding the changes and challenges that children face as they grow and develop, we can provide the necessary support, guidance, and resources to help them succeed. Whether it be in the classroom, at home, or in a healthcare setting, a solid understanding of child development is essential for promoting the well-being and success of all children.

# Chapter 3: Building Strong Parent-Child Relationships

## - Communication Strategies

Communication strategies refer to the methods and techniques used by individuals or organizations to convey information effectively to their intended audience. In today's fast-paced and interconnected world, effective communication has become essential for success in both personal and professional spheres. Whether it is a business trying to reach its customers, a student presenting a project, or a manager leading a team, the ability to communicate clearly and persuasively is crucial.

One key aspect of communication strategies is understanding the audience. Before you can effectively communicate a message, you need to know who you are speaking to. This involves considering factors such as their demographics, preferences, knowledge level, and potential biases. By understanding your audience, you can tailor your message in a way that is relevant and engaging to them. For example, if you are giving a presentation to a group of senior executives, you may want to focus on high-level strategic insights rather than getting bogged down in technical details.

Another important element of communication strategies is choosing the right channels. In today's digital age, there are numerous ways to communicate with others, including face-to-face interactions, phone calls, emails, social media, and video conferencing. Different channels have different strengths and weaknesses, so it is important to select the most appropriate one for your message. For instance, if you need to have a detailed discussion with a colleague, a face-to-face meeting might be more effective than exchanging emails back and forth.

When it comes to verbal communication, clarity is paramount. People are bombarded with information from all directions, so it is important to be concise and to the point. Avoid using jargon or technical language that may be confusing to your audience. Instead, use simple and straightforward language that is easy to understand. Furthermore, be mindful of your tone and body language, as these can greatly impact how your message is received. By speaking clearly, confidently, and respectfully, you can build trust and credibility with your audience.

In addition to verbal communication, nonverbal communication plays a crucial role in conveying messages effectively. Nonverbal cues such as facial expressions, gestures, and posture can provide valuable context and insight into how your words are being received. For example, maintaining eye contact and nodding in agreement can signal that you are engaged and attentive, while crossing your arms or fidgeting may indicate disinterest or discomfort. By paying attention to your nonverbal signals and adjusting them accordingly, you can enhance the effectiveness of your communication.

One of the most powerful communication strategies is active listening. Too often, people focus on what they want to say without truly listening to what others have to say. Active listening involves giving your full attention to the speaker, asking clarifying questions, and showing empathy and understanding. By demonstrating that you are genuinely interested in what the other person has to say, you can build trust, foster strong relationships, and ensure that your communication is two-way and interactive.

Lastly, feedback is a crucial component of effective communication strategies. Whether you are giving a presentation, having a meeting, or sending an email, it is important to solicit feedback from your audience to ensure that your message was understood and well-received. This can involve asking for input, conducting surveys, or simply observing the reactions of your audience. By incorporating feedback into your communication strategies, you can continuously improve and refine your message to better meet the needs and expectations of your audience. By understanding your audience, choosing the right channels, speaking clearly, using nonverbal cues, actively listening, and soliciting feedback, you can enhance the impact and effectiveness of your messages. Whether you are a business professional, student, or team leader, mastering these communication strategies can help you achieve your communication goals and build strong relationships with others.

# - Establishing Trust

Trust is a fundamental aspect of human relationships and plays a vital role in various aspects of our lives, from personal relationships to business interactions. Establishing trust is crucial in building strong and enduring relationships, as it forms the foundation upon which mutual respect, cooperation, and collaboration can thrive. Trust can be defined as the reliance or confidence placed in someone or something, based on the belief that they will act in a reliable, honest, and ethical manner. In essence, trust involves a level of vulnerability and willingness to rely on another person or entity, with the expectation that they will uphold their commitments and obligations.

There are several key factors that contribute to the establishment of trust in relationships. One of the most important factors is authenticity and transparency. Being honest, open, and genuine in your interactions with others creates a sense of authenticity, which can help build trust. People are more likely to trust someone who is transparent about their intentions, beliefs, and actions, as it signals that they have nothing to hide and can be trusted to act truthfully and ethically. In contrast, individuals who are deceptive, manipulative, or dishonest are likely to erode trust and damage relationships.

Another crucial factor in establishing trust is reliability and consistency. Trust is built over time through repeated interactions and experiences that demonstrate reliability and consistency in someone's behavior. People are more likely to trust someone who consistently follows through on their promises, meets their obligations, and acts predictably in different situations. Inconsistency, on the other hand, can breed doubt and uncertainty, undermining trust and creating a sense of instability in the relationship. Consistency in behavior, communication, and actions is therefore essential in building and maintaining trust.

Communication is also a key component in establishing trust in relationships. Effective communication involves listening, understanding, and responding to the needs, concerns, and emotions of others in a respectful and empathetic manner. Good communication skills can help foster mutual understanding, cooperation, and trust, by creating a safe and open space for honest and authentic dialogue. Clear, honest, and transparent communication can help clarify expectations, resolve conflicts, and build rapport, fostering a sense of trust and connection between individuals.

In addition to authenticity, reliability, consistency, and communication, integrity and ethical behavior are essential in establishing trust in relationships. Integrity involves acting in alignment with one's values, principles, and ethical standards, even when faced with challenges or temptations. Individuals who demonstrate integrity by consistently upholding their moral and ethical values are more likely to earn the trust and respect of others, as they are seen as trustworthy and reliable.

Trust is a dynamic and evolving process that requires ongoing effort, commitment, and investment from all parties involved. Building trust takes time and patience, as it involves establishing a strong foundation of mutual respect, understanding, and cooperation. Trust can be fragile and easily damaged, so it is important to nurture and protect it through consistent and authentic actions and communication. By practicing honesty, reliability, consistency, integrity, and ethical behavior in our interactions with others, we can build and maintain trust in our relationships, fostering mutual respect, collaboration, and cooperation.

## - Bonding Activities

Bonding activities are an essential component of building and maintaining strong relationships in both personal and professional settings. These activities provide opportunities for individuals to connect on a deeper level, foster trust and camaraderie, and create a sense of unity within a group. Whether it is with friends, family members, colleagues, or peers, engaging in bonding activities can lead to increased communication, enhanced teamwork, and a more positive overall environment.

One of the key benefits of bonding activities is the opportunity they provide for individuals to get to know one another on a more personal level. By participating in activities outside of the usual routine, such as team-building exercises, recreational outings, or social events, people have the chance to share experiences, interests, and stories that they may not otherwise have the opportunity to discuss. This can lead to a deeper understanding and appreciation of one another, ultimately strengthening the bonds between individuals and creating a more cohesive group dynamic.

In addition to fostering personal connections, bonding activities also help to build trust and camaraderie among participants. When people engage in activities that require teamwork, communication, and cooperation, they must rely on one another to achieve a common goal. This shared experience can create a sense of mutual respect and trust, as individuals see firsthand how their colleagues, friends, or family members contribute to the group's success. As trust and camaraderie grow, so too does the sense of unity within the group, leading to a more positive and supportive environment for all involved.

Furthermore, bonding activities can have a significant impact on the overall effectiveness of a team or group. When individuals have strong relationships and a sense of unity with one another, they are more likely to communicate openly and honestly, collaborate effectively, and work together towards common goals. This can lead to increased productivity, creativity, and innovation, as team members feel comfortable sharing ideas, challenging one another, and working together to problem-solve and overcome obstacles. Ultimately, bonding activities can help to create a cohesive and high-performing team that is better equipped to achieve success in their endeavors.

It is important to note that bonding activities can take many different forms, depending on the nature of the group and the goals of the activity. For example, team-building exercises may involve problem-solving challenges, communication games, or physical activities that require cooperation and coordination. Recreational outings, such as group hikes, sports games, or cultural excursions, can provide opportunities for relaxation and enjoyment while also promoting bonding and social connection. Social events, such as dinners, parties, or outings to movies or concerts, offer a more informal setting for individuals to unwind, socialize, and strengthen relationships in a relaxed and enjoyable environment. By providing opportunities for individuals to connect on a deeper level, foster trust and camaraderie, and create a sense of unity within a group, these activities can lead to increased communication, enhanced teamwork, and a more positive overall environment. Whether it is through team-building exercises, recreational outings, or social events, engaging in bonding activities can help to strengthen relationships, build trust and camaraderie, and create a more cohesive and high-performing group. Ultimately, bonding activities are an essential tool for fostering positive relationships and promoting success in all areas of life.

# Chapter 4: Effective Discipline Techniques

## - Positive Reinforcement

Positive reinforcement is a powerful tool in shaping behavior and promoting learning in various settings, including schools, workplaces, and homes. It is a technique that involves the presentation of a desirable stimulus or reward following a desired behavior, with the goal of increasing the likelihood that the behavior will be repeated in the future. Positive reinforcement is based on the principles of operant conditioning, a theory developed by psychologist B. F. Skinner.

In operant conditioning, behavior is influenced by its consequences. When a behavior is followed by a pleasant consequence, such as praise, a reward, or some other form of positive reinforcement, it is more likely to be repeated in the future. Positive reinforcement can take many forms, including verbal praise, stickers, tokens, points, privileges, or tangible rewards such as toys or treats. The key is that the reinforcement must be something that the individual finds rewarding and motivating.

One of the key benefits of positive reinforcement is that it can be used to shape behavior in a way that is both effective and humane. Instead of relying on punishment or negative consequences to eliminate unwanted behaviors, positive reinforcement focuses on promoting desired behaviors through the use of rewards and incentives. This not only helps to create a more positive and supportive environment, but it also helps individuals to develop new skills and habits in a way that is more sustainable and long-lasting.

Positive reinforcement can be particularly effective in educational settings, where it can be used to encourage students to engage in learning activities, participate in class discussions, complete assignments, and follow classroom rules. By providing students with positive feedback, rewards, and recognition for their efforts and achievements, teachers can help to motivate them to work hard, stay focused, and achieve their academic goals. Positive reinforcement can also help to build students' self-esteem and confidence, as they receive validation and praise for their accomplishments.

In the workplace, positive reinforcement can be used to motivate employees, improve productivity, and enhance job satisfaction. By recognizing and rewarding employees for their hard work, dedication, and contributions to the organization, managers can create a more positive and supportive work environment. This can lead to increased morale, engagement, and job performance, as employees feel valued, appreciated, and motivated to do their best.

At home, positive reinforcement can be used to promote desired behaviors in children, such as completing chores, following rules, and being respectful to others. By using rewards, praise, and privileges to reinforce positive behaviors, parents can help their children learn important life skills, develop good habits, and build strong relationships. Positive reinforcement can also help to strengthen the bond between parents and children, as it fosters a sense of love, trust, and cooperation.

While positive reinforcement is a valuable tool for promoting learning and behavior change, it is important to use it effectively and appropriately. In order for positive reinforcement to be successful, it must be delivered consistently, immediately following the desired behavior, and in a way that is meaningful and rewarding to the individual. It is also important to vary the types of reinforcement used, in order to maintain motivation and prevent habituation. Additionally, positive reinforcement should be used in conjunction with other teaching strategies and behavior management techniques, such as clear expectations, modeling, and consequences for inappropriate behavior. By providing individuals with rewards, recognition, and incentives for their efforts and achievements, positive reinforcement can help to motivate them to work hard, stay focused, and achieve their goals. Whether in the classroom, the workplace, or at home, positive reinforcement can be a valuable tool for creating a supportive and encouraging environment, where individuals can thrive and succeed. By understanding the principles of positive reinforcement and applying them in a thoughtful and deliberate manner, we can help to create a more positive and productive world for ourselves and those around us.

# - Setting Boundaries

Setting boundaries is an important aspect of maintaining healthy relationships and promoting personal well-being. Boundaries serve as guidelines for how we expect to be treated by others and how we will treat them in return. By clearly defining our boundaries, we can prevent misunderstandings, reduce conflict, and foster mutual respect in our interactions.

One key aspect of setting boundaries is recognizing and honoring our own needs and limits. It is important to be aware of what makes us feel comfortable or uncomfortable, and to communicate this to others in a clear and assertive manner. This can involve setting limits on the amount of time or energy we are willing to give to certain people or activities, as well as establishing expectations for how we expect to be treated in different situations.

In addition to knowing and communicating our own boundaries, it is also important to be respectful of the boundaries of others. This means listening to and acknowledging their needs and limits, and not pushing them to do things that make them feel uncomfortable or go against their values. By being mindful of the boundaries of others, we can build trust and strengthen our relationships.

Setting boundaries is not always easy, especially if we have a history of people-pleasing or have difficulty asserting ourselves. It may require practice and self-awareness to become more comfortable with setting and enforcing boundaries. However, the benefits of setting boundaries are well worth the effort. By clearly defining our limits and expectations, we can create a sense of safety and predictability in our relationships, which can lead to greater trust, intimacy, and mutual respect.

There are several strategies that can help us set and maintain healthy boundaries in our relationships. One key strategy is to be clear and direct in our communication. This means clearly stating our needs, limits, and expectations in a respectful and assertive manner. It can be helpful to use "I" statements to express our feelings and needs without blaming or accusing others. For example, instead of saying "You always make me feel guilty when I say no," we can say "I feel uncomfortable when I am pressured to do something I don't want to do. "

Another important strategy is to practice self-care and self-compassion. Setting boundaries can be difficult, especially if we are used to putting others' needs before our own. It is important to prioritize our own well-being and to give ourselves permission to say no when we need to. This may involve setting aside time for ourselves to rest, relax, and recharge, as well as seeking support from friends, family, or a therapist when needed.

It is also important to be consistent and firm in enforcing our boundaries. While it may be tempting to give in to pressure or guilt from others, it is important to remember that our boundaries are there to protect us and to promote healthy relationships. This may require us to say no to certain requests or to distance ourselves from people who consistently disrespect our boundaries. By being firm and consistent in enforcing our boundaries, we can send a clear message that we value ourselves and expect to be treated with respect. By recognizing and honoring our own needs and limits, being respectful of the boundaries of others, and using clear and direct communication, we can create a sense of safety and respect in our interactions. While setting boundaries may require practice and self-awareness, the benefits of doing so are well worth the effort. By prioritizing our own well-being and enforcing our boundaries with consistency and firmness, we can cultivate strong, meaningful relationships built on trust, respect, and mutual understanding.

## - Consistency in Discipline

Consistency in discipline is a crucial aspect of maintaining order and promoting positive behavior in any organization or group setting. It involves applying the same set of rules and consequences consistently to all individuals, regardless of their background or position within the group. By enforcing discipline consistently, leaders can create a fair and transparent environment where everyone knows what is expected of them and what the consequences are for not meeting those expectations.

Consistency in discipline is essential for several reasons. First and foremost, it promotes fairness and equity within the group. When rules and consequences are applied inconsistently, it can create a sense of favoritism or injustice among members, leading to resentment and tension within the group. By treating everyone equally and holding all individuals accountable to the same standards, leaders can create a sense of trust and respect among group members.

Furthermore, consistency in discipline helps to establish clear expectations and promote accountability. When individuals know that the rules will be enforced consistently and that there will be consequences for their actions, they are more likely to adhere to those rules and take responsibility for their behavior. This, in turn, can help to prevent misconduct and promote a positive and respectful atmosphere within the group.

Consistency in discipline also helps to create a sense of stability and predictability within the organization. When rules and consequences are applied inconsistently, it can create confusion and uncertainty among group members, leading to a lack of trust and cohesion within the group. By enforcing discipline consistently, leaders can create a sense of order and structure within the organization, which can help to promote a sense of unity and teamwork among group members.

In order to maintain consistency in discipline, leaders must establish clear and transparent rules and consequences that apply to all individuals within the organization. These rules should be communicated effectively to all group members and should be applied consistently and fairly to all individuals. Leaders should also be consistent in their enforcement of the rules, not playing favorites or making exceptions for certain individuals.

It is also important for leaders to be mindful of the impact of their own behavior on the consistency of discipline within the organization. Leaders must lead by example and demonstrate a commitment to upholding the rules and consequences set forth for the group. When leaders fail to adhere to the same standards that they expect from others, it can undermine the consistency of discipline within the organization and erode trust and respect among group members. By applying the same set of rules and consequences consistently to all individuals, leaders can create a fair and transparent environment where everyone knows what is expected of them and what the consequences are for not meeting those expectations. Consistency in discipline promotes fairness, accountability, stability, and unity within the organization and helps to create a positive and respectful atmosphere where all individuals can thrive and succeed.

# Chapter 5: Encouraging Independence and Responsibility

## - Age-Appropriate Tasks

Age-appropriate tasks refer to activities or responsibilities that are suitable for a child's developmental stage and age. These tasks vary depending on the child's physical, cognitive, and emotional abilities, as well as their interests and preferences. It is important for parents, caregivers, and educators to be mindful of age-appropriate tasks when assigning responsibilities to children, as this can enhance their sense of independence, confidence, and self-esteem.

For infants and toddlers, age-appropriate tasks may include simple activities such as picking up toys, putting away books, or helping to dress themselves. These tasks help young children develop fine motor skills, independence, and a sense of responsibility. It is important for caregivers to provide gentle guidance and support as children learn to complete these tasks on their own.

As children grow older, age-appropriate tasks become more complex and challenging. For preschool-aged children, tasks such as setting the table, feeding pets, or helping with simple chores around the house can be suitable. These tasks help children develop a sense of responsibility, cooperation, and teamwork. It is important for parents and caregivers to provide clear instructions and positive reinforcement to encourage children to complete these tasks.

For school-aged children, age-appropriate tasks may include more complex responsibilities such as doing homework independently, helping with meal preparation, or taking care of their personal belongings. These tasks help children develop time management skills, organization, and independence. It is important for parents and educators to set clear expectations and provide support as children learn to take on more responsibilities.

Teenagers can also benefit from age-appropriate tasks that challenge them to develop important life skills such as budgeting, time management, and decision-making. Tasks such as managing their own finances, volunteering in the community, or taking on a part-time job can help teenagers develop independence, resilience, and a sense of purpose. It is important for parents and educators to provide guidance and support as teenagers navigate these new responsibilities. By assigning tasks that are suitable for a child's age and abilities, parents, caregivers, and educators can help children build important skills, foster independence, and promote self-confidence. It is essential to be mindful of children's individual needs and preferences when assigning tasks, and to provide support and encouragement as they learn and grow. By incorporating age-appropriate tasks into children's daily routines, we can help them become capable, confident, and responsible individuals.

## - Teaching Life Skills

Teaching life skills is a crucial aspect of education that goes beyond traditional academic subjects. Life skills are the everyday abilities that allow individuals to navigate the challenges of daily life and achieve their personal goals. These skills encompass a wide range of competencies, including communication, problem-solving, decision-making, time management, and interpersonal relationships. By teaching life skills, educators can empower students to succeed in both their academic pursuits and their future careers.

One of the key benefits of teaching life skills is that it prepares students for the real world. In today's fast-paced and dynamic society, individuals need more than just academic knowledge to thrive in their personal and professional lives. By equipping students with essential life skills, educators can help them develop the resilience, adaptability, and self-confidence needed to overcome obstacles and seize opportunities. These skills are not only valuable in the workplace but also in personal relationships and daily decision-making.

Furthermore, teaching life skills can enhance students' social and emotional well-being. Studies have shown that individuals who possess strong life skills are more likely to have better mental health and lower levels of stress and anxiety. By teaching students how to manage their emotions, communicate effectively, and build healthy relationships, educators can promote a positive school environment and empower students to navigate the complexities of social interactions with confidence and empathy. Life skills education can also help students develop a sense of self-awareness and self-acceptance, which are essential for personal growth and fulfillment.

Another important aspect of teaching life skills is fostering critical thinking and problem-solving abilities. Life skills education encourages students to think outside the box, analyze situations from different perspectives, and make informed decisions based on evidence and reasoning. By providing students with opportunities to tackle real-world challenges and learn from their mistakes, educators can help them develop essential problem-solving skills that are crucial for success in both academic and professional settings. Additionally, teaching life skills can enhance students' creativity and innovation, enabling them to envision new solutions to complex problems and adapt to changing circumstances.

In addition to enhancing students' academic and social-emotional development, teaching life skills can also promote lifelong learning and personal growth. Life skills education instills a growth mindset in students, encouraging them to embrace challenges, learn from failures, and continuously improve themselves. By teaching students how to set goals, plan effectively, and track their progress, educators can foster a sense of purpose and direction in their lives. Life skills education also promotes self-reflection and self-assessment, enabling students to identify their strengths and weaknesses and take proactive steps to improve themselves. By imparting essential competencies such as communication, problem-solving, decision-making, and time management, educators can empower students to navigate the complexities of the modern world with confidence and resilience. Life skills education not only enhances students' academic performance but also fosters their social-emotional well-being, critical thinking abilities, and personal growth. By integrating life skills education into the curriculum, educators can equip students with the tools they need to thrive in a rapidly changing and competitive society.

# - Empowering Children

Empowering children is a crucial aspect of their development and growth. It involves providing them with the necessary tools, resources, and opportunities to thrive and reach their full potential. By empowering children, we are enabling them to build confidence, self-esteem, and a sense of agency in their own lives. This is essential for their overall well-being and success in the future.

One of the key ways to empower children is through education. Education plays a vital role in shaping the minds and lives of young individuals. By providing children with access to quality education, we are equipping them with the knowledge and skills they need to navigate the world around them. Education empowers children to think critically, solve problems, and make informed decisions. It also opens up a world of opportunities and possibilities for them, enabling them to pursue their passions and interests.

In addition to education, it is important to empower children by fostering a supportive and nurturing environment for them to grow and thrive. This includes providing them with love, encouragement, and positive reinforcement. By creating a safe and loving space for children to express themselves and explore their capabilities, we are helping them develop a strong sense of self-worth and confidence. This, in turn, empowers them to take on challenges and overcome obstacles with resilience and determination.

Furthermore, empowering children also involves helping them develop essential life skills that will serve them well in the future. This includes teaching them how to communicate effectively, manage their emotions, build healthy relationships, and make responsible choices. By instilling these skills in children from a young age, we are empowering them to become independent, self-reliant individuals who are capable of navigating the complexities of adulthood.

It is also important to empower children by encouraging them to take risks and pursue their passions. By fostering a sense of curiosity and creativity in children, we are empowering them to explore new ideas, try new things, and push beyond their comfort zones. This not only helps them develop a growth mindset but also instills in them a sense of purpose and fulfillment. By encouraging children to follow their dreams and pursue their interests, we are empowering them to realize their full potential and make a positive impact on the world around them.

Additionally, empowering children involves listening to their voices and valuing their opinions and perspectives. Children are unique individuals with their own thoughts, feelings, and ideas. By actively listening to children and taking their input into consideration, we are empowering them to assert themselves and participate actively in decision-making processes that affect their lives. This not only helps them develop a sense of autonomy and agency but also fosters a culture of respect and inclusivity. By providing children with access to quality education, a supportive environment, essential life skills, and the encouragement to pursue their passions, we are empowering them to thrive and reach their full potential. Empowered children are confident, capable, and resilient individuals who are prepared to navigate life's challenges and make a positive impact on the world around them. As educators, parents, and caregivers, it is our responsibility to empower children and support them in their journey towards success and fulfillment.

# Chapter 6: Creating a Positive Parenting Environment

## - Setting a Good Example

One of the most important aspects of leadership and influence is setting a good example for others to follow. Whether in the professional world, academic settings, or personal relationships, people look up to those who demonstrate integrity, transparency, and authenticity in their actions and behaviors. Setting a good example is not just about telling others what to do; it's about showing them through your own actions how to navigate challenges, make ethical decisions, and strive for excellence in all aspects of life.

In a professional context, setting a good example starts with upholding high standards of performance and behavior. This means being punctual, prepared, and focused on the task at hand. It also means treating colleagues, subordinates, and superiors with respect and professionalism, even in difficult or challenging situations. By demonstrating a strong work ethic, positive attitude, and commitment to excellence, you inspire those around you to do the same and create a culture of accountability and success within your team or organization.

In academic settings, setting a good example involves not just excelling in your coursework, but also demonstrating a passion for learning and a commitment to intellectual curiosity. This means actively participating in class discussions, seeking out opportunities for extra study or research, and engaging with professors and classmates in a respectful and collaborative manner. By taking your academic responsibilities seriously and approaching your studies with dedication and enthusiasm, you set a positive example for others to follow and create a dynamic and stimulating learning environment that benefits everyone.

In personal relationships, setting a good example means embodying the values and principles that are important to you, such as honesty, kindness, and empathy. It means being a good listener, supporting others in their goals and aspirations, and being a reliable and trustworthy friend or partner. By demonstrating integrity, authenticity, and compassion in your interactions with others, you build strong and meaningful connections that enrich your life and the lives of those around you.

Ultimately, setting a good example is about leading by example and inspiring others to be their best selves. It's about showing through your actions and behaviors what it means to be a person of integrity, character, and conviction. By consistently demonstrating honesty, fairness, and respect in all aspects of your life, you not only earn the trust and respect of those around you, but also create a positive ripple effect that influences others to follow in your footsteps. Whether in the workplace, the classroom, or your personal relationships, setting a good example is a powerful tool for building trust, fostering collaboration, and creating a culture of excellence and integrity.

# - Providing Emotional Support

Providing emotional support is a crucial aspect of helping individuals navigate through difficult times and challenges in their lives. It involves being present for someone in a nonjudgmental and empathetic way, offering comfort, reassurance, and understanding. Emotional support can come in many forms, such as listening actively, offering words of encouragement, showing empathy, providing physical gestures of comfort, and being a source of stability and reassurance.

One of the key components of providing emotional support is active listening. This means being fully present and engaged in the conversation, not just hearing the words that are being said but truly understanding the emotions behind them. It involves giving your full attention to the person, making eye contact, nodding, and asking clarifying questions to show that you are actively engaged in the conversation. Active listening helps the person feel heard and understood, which can be particularly comforting in times of distress.

Another important aspect of providing emotional support is offering words of encouragement and reassurance. This can involve expressing belief in the person's abilities and strengths, reminding them of past successes, and offering hope for the future. It is important to choose your words carefully and to be sincere in your encouragement, as insincere or empty platitudes can do more harm than good. Encouraging words can help boost the person's confidence and self-esteem, giving them the motivation they need to face their challenges head-on.

Showing empathy is another essential component of providing emotional support. Empathy involves putting yourself in the other person's shoes, trying to understand their perspective, and validating their feelings. It is about being sensitive to the person's emotions and showing that you care about their well-being. Empathy can be expressed through words, gestures, or simply being there for the person when they need a listening ear. By demonstrating empathy, you are showing the person that you understand and care about their struggles, which can create a sense of connection and comfort.

Providing physical gestures of comfort can also be a powerful way to offer emotional support. This can include giving hugs, holding hands, or offering a shoulder to cry on. Physical touch can be incredibly soothing and comforting, as it can help reduce stress levels and release feel-good hormones like oxytocin. Of course, it is important to respect the other person's boundaries and only offer physical comfort if they are comfortable with it. Physical gestures of comfort can help create a sense of closeness and connection, providing a comforting presence in times of need.

Being a source of stability and reassurance is another important aspect of providing emotional support. When someone is going through a challenging time, they may feel overwhelmed, anxious, or uncertain about the future. By being a stable and reassuring presence in their life, you can help them feel grounded, secure, and supported. This involves being reliable, consistent, and trustworthy, and offering a sense of predictability and dependability. By providing stability and reassurance, you can help the person feel safe and secure, allowing them to navigate through their difficulties with more confidence and resilience. It involves active listening, offering words of encouragement, showing empathy, providing physical gestures of comfort, and being a source of stability and reassurance. By being present for someone in a nonjudgmental and empathetic way, you can help them feel heard, understood, and supported.

Emotional support is a powerful tool that can help individuals cope with their emotions, build resilience, and overcome adversity. By offering emotional support to those in need, you can make a positive impact on their well-being and help them navigate through life's challenges with strength and courage.

## - Encouraging Creativity and Exploration

Encouraging creativity and exploration is essential for personal growth, learning, innovation, and problem-solving. Creativity involves the ability to generate new ideas, concepts, or solutions that are original and valuable. It is a crucial skill in today's rapidly changing and complex world, where traditional approaches may no longer be effective. Exploration, on the other hand, involves the process of discovering, trying out new things, and stepping out of one's comfort zone. It is through exploration that we expand our knowledge, skills, and experiences, fostering personal development and growth.

One way to encourage creativity and exploration is to create an environment that is supportive, safe, and conducive to taking risks. People are more likely to be creative and explore new ideas when they feel comfortable and free from judgment. This means fostering a culture of open communication, collaboration, and experimentation. Encouraging individuals to share their thoughts, take initiative, and challenge the status quo can lead to breakthrough ideas and innovative solutions. By creating a safe space for creativity and exploration, organizations can tap into the diverse perspectives and talents of their employees, driving growth and success.

Another way to foster creativity and exploration is to provide opportunities for learning, growth, and development. Continuous learning is essential for personal and professional growth, and it can lead to increased creativity and innovation. By offering training programs, workshops, and resources that support skill development, organizations can empower employees to explore new ideas and approaches. Encouraging lifelong learning and investing in personal growth can boost creativity, enhance problem-solving skills, and foster a culture of innovation within the organization.

In addition to creating a supportive environment and promoting learning opportunities, it is essential to provide resources and tools that facilitate creativity and exploration. This could include access to technology, creative spaces, materials, and resources that support experimentation and idea generation. Providing employees with the necessary tools and resources can enable them to explore new possibilities, collaborate with others, and bring their ideas to life. By investing in resources that support creativity and exploration, organizations can empower employees to think outside the box and drive innovation.

Furthermore, leaders play a crucial role in encouraging creativity and exploration within their teams and organizations. Leaders should set a positive example by embracing creativity, taking risks, and encouraging others to do the same. By demonstrating a willingness to explore new ideas and approaches, leaders can inspire their teams to think creatively and push beyond their limits. Effective leaders also provide guidance, support, and feedback to help individuals navigate the creative process and explore new avenues. By fostering a culture of creativity and exploration, leaders can empower their teams to unlock their potential and drive innovation. By creating a supportive environment, providing learning opportunities, offering resources and tools, and empowering leaders to lead by example, organizations can foster a culture of creativity and exploration. This can lead to increased employee engagement, satisfaction, and productivity, as well as drive innovation and success. Ultimately, by encouraging creativity and exploration, organizations can unlock the full potential of their employees and achieve their goals.

# Chapter 7: Managing Stress and Self-Care

## - Balancing Parenting and Personal Needs

Parenting is undoubtedly one of the most important and rewarding roles a person can undertake in their lifetime. The care and well-being of our children are paramount, and most parents will go to great lengths to ensure their children are happy, healthy, and thriving. However, while parenting is a fulfilling and enriching experience, it can also be demanding and all-consuming at times. As parents, we are constantly juggling the needs and demands of our children with our own personal needs and desires. Balancing parenting and personal needs can be a delicate and challenging task, but with careful planning and self-awareness, it is possible to find a healthy balance that benefits both ourselves and our children.

One of the key challenges in balancing parenting and personal needs is finding the time and energy to devote to both aspects of our lives. Parenting is a full-time job, with no days off or sick leave. From the moment we wake up in the morning until we go to bed at night, our children depend on us for their care and support. This leaves little time for us to focus on our own needs and interests. Many parents find themselves sacrificing their own well-being in order to meet the needs of their children, leading to burnout and resentment. It is important for parents to recognize that taking care of themselves is not selfish, but essential for their own mental and physical health. By prioritizing self-care and carving out time for their personal needs, parents can replenish their energy and feel more fulfilled in their role as caregivers.

Another challenge in balancing parenting and personal needs is the guilt and pressure that many parents feel when they prioritize themselves over their children. Society often glorifies the self-sacrificing parent who puts their children's needs above their own at all times. While it is true that children need love, attention, and support from their parents, it is also important for parents to take care of themselves in order to be effective caregivers. Parents who neglect their own needs and well-being are more likely to become stressed, irritable, and resentful, which can negatively impact their relationship with their children. It is important for parents to let go of the guilt and embrace the idea that taking care of themselves benefits their children as well. By prioritizing self-care and personal fulfillment, parents can model healthy behavior for their children and create a more harmonious and balanced family dynamic.

One strategy for balancing parenting and personal needs is to establish clear boundaries and priorities. In order to find a healthy balance between caring for our children and caring for ourselves, it is important to set boundaries and prioritize our time and energy. This may involve saying no to certain commitments or obligations that drain our resources and detract from our well-being. It may also involve delegating tasks and responsibilities to other family members or seeking outside help when needed. By being intentional and strategic with our time and energy, we can create a more efficient and fulfilling lifestyle that benefits both ourselves and our children. It is important to recognize that it is not only okay, but necessary, to prioritize ourselves and our needs in order to be the best parents we can be.

Another important aspect of balancing parenting and personal needs is communication and support. Parenting can be isolating at times, and many parents feel overwhelmed and alone in their struggles. It is important for parents to reach out to others for support and guidance, whether it be friends, family members, or professionals. By sharing our experiences and challenges with others, we can gain new perspectives and insight that can help us navigate the complexities of parenthood. It is also important for parents to communicate openly and honestly with their children about their needs and limitations. By involving our children in the decision-making process and setting realistic expectations, we can create a more supportive and understanding family environment that values the needs of all its members. While parenting is a demanding and all-consuming role, it is important for parents to prioritize their own well-being in order to be effective caregivers. By setting boundaries, prioritizing self-care, and seeking support when needed, parents can create a more harmonious and balanced lifestyle that benefits both themselves and their children. It is important for parents to let go of the guilt and pressure to be perfect, and instead focus on creating a nurturing and supportive environment that values the needs and well-being of all family members. By taking care of ourselves, we can better care for our children and create a more fulfilling and rewarding parenting experience for everyone involved.

# - Coping Strategies for Stress

Stress is an inevitable part of life that we all experience at some point or another. Whether it's from work, relationships, or other responsibilities, stress can take a toll on our mental and physical health if not managed effectively. Coping strategies for stress are essential tools that can help us navigate through difficult times and come out stronger on the other side.

One of the most effective coping strategies for managing stress is practicing mindfulness. Mindfulness is the practice of being fully present and aware of your thoughts, feelings, and surroundings without judgment. By focusing on the present moment rather than worrying about the future or dwelling on the past, you can reduce feelings of anxiety and stress. Mindfulness can be practiced through meditation, deep breathing exercises, or simply taking a few moments to pause and pay attention to your surroundings.

Another helpful coping strategy for stress is maintaining a healthy lifestyle. This includes eating a balanced diet, getting regular exercise, and prioritizing sleep. Research has shown that regular physical activity can help reduce stress levels by releasing endorphins, which are neurotransmitters that act as natural painkillers and mood elevators. Additionally, getting enough sleep is crucial for managing stress, as lack of sleep can impair cognitive function and increase feelings of irritability and anxiety.

Seeking support from others is also an important coping strategy for stress. Talking to friends, family members, or a therapist about what you're going through can provide comfort and perspective. It's important to remember that it's okay to ask for help when you need it and that you don't have to go through difficult times alone. In addition to talking to loved ones, joining a support group or seeking counseling can also be beneficial in helping you cope with stress in a healthy way.

Engaging in activities that bring you joy and relaxation is another effective coping strategy for managing stress. Whether it's reading a book, taking a walk in nature, or listening to music, finding time to do things that make you happy can help distract you from stressful thoughts and give you a much-needed mental break. Engaging in creative outlets such as painting, writing, or playing an instrument can also be therapeutic and provide an emotional release.

Lastly, practicing self-care is an essential coping strategy for stress. This includes setting boundaries, saying no to things that overwhelm you, and taking time for yourself to recharge. It's important to prioritize your own well-being and make self-care a non-negotiable part of your routine. This can include activities such as taking a relaxing bath, practicing gratitude, or treating yourself to something you enjoy. By taking care of yourself, you can better manage stress and build resilience to navigate through challenging times. By practicing mindfulness, maintaining a healthy lifestyle, seeking support from others, engaging in activities that bring you joy, and practicing self-care, you can effectively manage stress and build resilience for the future. Remember that it's okay to ask for help when you need it and that taking care of yourself is a priority. By implementing these coping strategies into your daily routine, you can better cope with stress and live a happier, healthier life.

# - Importance of Self-Care for Parents

Self-care is a term that is often associated with indulgence or selfishness, but in reality, it is a crucial component of overall well-being. This is especially true for parents, who are often so consumed with caring for their children and tending to their needs that they neglect their own. However, it is essential for parents to prioritize self-care in order to maintain their physical, emotional, and mental health. By taking care of themselves, parents are better able to take care of their children and be present and engaged in their lives.

One of the key reasons why self-care is important for parents is that it helps to prevent burnout. Parenting is a demanding and relentless job, and it can be easy to become overwhelmed by the constant demands and responsibilities. Without taking time for themselves, parents can quickly become exhausted and depleted, making it difficult for them to effectively care for their children. By prioritizing self-care, parents can recharge their batteries and replenish their energy, allowing them to approach parenting with renewed vigor and enthusiasm.

Self-care also plays a crucial role in promoting mental health and emotional well-being. Parenthood can be a rollercoaster of emotions, from the joy and pride of watching your children grow and develop to the frustration and stress of dealing with tantrums and meltdowns. It is normal for parents to experience a wide range of emotions, but it is important for them to have healthy coping mechanisms in place to manage these feelings. Engaging in self-care activities such as exercise, meditation, or spending time with friends can provide parents with an outlet for stress and help them to maintain a positive mindset.

In addition to preventing burnout and promoting mental health, self-care is also important for parents to set a positive example for their children. Children learn by example, and when they see their parents prioritizing self-care and taking care of themselves, they are more likely to develop healthy habits and attitudes towards self-care as they grow older. By demonstrating the importance of self-care to their children, parents are instilling in them the value of self-love and self-respect, which are essential qualities for a happy and fulfilling life.

Furthermore, self-care can help parents to cultivate a greater sense of balance and equilibrium in their lives. Parenthood can often feel all-consuming, with parents constantly juggling the demands of work, family, and personal life. This can leave little time for self-care and relaxation, leading to feelings of stress and overwhelm. By making self-care a priority, parents can create a sense of balance and harmony in their lives, allowing them to better manage their time and energy and prioritize what is truly important to them.

Self-care is not a luxury or a selfish indulgence, but rather a necessary component of overall well-being for parents. By taking the time to care for themselves, parents can prevent burnout, promote mental health and emotional well-being, set a positive example for their children, and cultivate a sense of balance and equilibrium in their lives. In the hectic and demanding world of parenting, self-care is not only important, but essential for parents to thrive and be able to give their best to their children. So, let us all take a moment to pause, breathe, and prioritize self-care in our lives as parents.

# Chapter 8: Supporting Mental Health and Well-being

## - Recognizing Signs of Mental Health Issues

Mental health issues are a prevalent and often misunderstood aspect of overall well-being. It is crucial to recognize the signs of mental health issues in order to provide timely support and resources for those who may be struggling. By understanding common indicators and symptoms, individuals can better identify when someone may be in need of assistance and intervention. This can ultimately lead to improved mental health outcomes and a better quality of life for those experiencing mental health challenges.

One of the key signs of mental health issues is changes in behavior. This can manifest in a variety of ways, such as increased isolation, irritability, mood swings, or changes in sleep patterns. Individuals may also exhibit a loss of interest in activities they once enjoyed, or have difficulty concentrating or making decisions. These behavioral changes can be indicative of underlying mental health issues, such as depression, anxiety, or other mood disorders. It is important to pay attention to these changes in behavior and seek help if necessary.

Another common sign of mental health issues is changes in emotions. Individuals experiencing mental health issues may exhibit intense or prolonged feelings of sadness, hopelessness, or despair. They may also experience heightened levels of anxiety, fear, or worry. It is important to recognize and validate these emotions, as they can be indicators of underlying mental health issues that require attention and support. Open communication and empathy are key in helping individuals navigate and process their emotions in a healthy and constructive manner.

Physical symptoms can also be a sign of mental health issues. These can include changes in appetite, weight loss or gain, fatigue, or unexplained aches and pains.

Individuals may also exhibit changes in their personal hygiene or appearance, as well as physical restlessness or agitation. These physical symptoms can be manifestations of underlying mental health issues, such as stress, trauma, or other psychological factors. It is crucial to address these physical symptoms alongside emotional and behavioral signs in order to provide holistic support and care for individuals experiencing mental health challenges.

Cognitive symptoms can also be indicative of mental health issues. Individuals may experience difficulties with memory, concentration, or decision-making, which can impact their daily functioning and overall well-being. They may also exhibit excessive worrying, racing thoughts, or difficulty controlling their thoughts. These cognitive symptoms can be signs of mental health issues such as anxiety disorders, depression, or other cognitive challenges. It is important to address these cognitive symptoms and provide appropriate support and resources to help individuals manage and cope with their mental health issues.

Social changes can also signal mental health issues. Individuals may exhibit changes in their relationships, such as withdrawal from social interactions, conflict with others, or difficulties in communication. They may also experience feelings of loneliness, isolation, or disconnection from others. These social changes can be indicative of underlying mental health issues that impact how individuals interact with and relate to others. It is important to provide a supportive and understanding environment for individuals experiencing social changes as a result of their mental health issues. By understanding common indicators and symptoms, individuals can better identify when someone may be in need of assistance and intervention. It is important to pay attention to changes in behavior, emotions, physical symptoms, cognitive symptoms, and social changes in order to provide holistic care for those experiencing mental health challenges. By addressing these signs of mental health issues with empathy, understanding, and support, we can help promote mental well-being and improve the overall quality of life for individuals in need.

# - Seeking Professional Help

Seeking professional help is an important decision that can greatly improve one's mental health and overall well-being. In today's society, there is a growing awareness of the importance of mental health and the need to address any issues that may arise. Professional help can come in many forms, including therapy, counseling, and psychiatric care. These professionals are trained to provide guidance, support, and treatment for a wide range of mental health issues, from anxiety and depression to more serious conditions such as bipolar disorder and schizophrenia.

One of the main reasons to seek professional help is to gain a better understanding of your own mental health and to develop coping strategies to deal with any issues that may arise. Therapy and counseling can provide a safe and confidential space to explore your thoughts and feelings, and to work through any emotional struggles that you may be facing. A trained therapist or counselor can offer insights and perspectives that can help you gain a deeper understanding of yourself and your behavior, and can help you develop healthier ways of coping with stress and challenges.

Another important reason to seek professional help is to receive a proper diagnosis and treatment for any mental health conditions that you may be experiencing. A licensed psychiatrist or psychologist can assess your symptoms, provide a diagnosis, and recommend an appropriate course of treatment, which may include therapy, medication, or a combination of both. Getting the right diagnosis and treatment plan is crucial for managing and improving your mental health, and can make a significant difference in your quality of life.

It is also important to seek professional help if you are experiencing severe or persistent symptoms of mental illness, such as suicidal thoughts, self-harm behavior, or severe anxiety and depression. These symptoms can be signs of a serious mental health crisis that requires immediate intervention. A mental health professional can provide crisis intervention and support, and can help you access the resources and services you need to stay safe and get the help you need.

Seeking professional help can also be beneficial for those who are struggling with interpersonal relationships, work-related stress, or other life challenges.

A trained therapist or counselor can help you develop communication skills, set boundaries, and work through conflicts in a healthy and constructive way. Therapy can also help you identify and change negative patterns of thinking and behavior that may be causing difficulties in your relationships or at work, and can help you develop more positive and adaptive coping skills.

It is important to remember that seeking professional help is not a sign of weakness, but rather a sign of strength and self-awareness. It takes courage to acknowledge that you may need help, and to take the necessary steps to reach out and ask for support. Whether you are struggling with a mental health issue, a relationship problem, or a life challenge, seeking professional help can be a valuable and empowering step toward healing and growth. Remember, you are not alone, and there are professionals who are ready and willing to help you on your journey to better mental health and well-being.

## - Promoting Emotional Wellness

Promoting emotional wellness involves developing self-awareness, managing emotions effectively, and cultivating positive relationships with others.

One of the first steps in promoting emotional wellness is to cultivate self-awareness. This involves recognizing and accepting one's own emotions, thoughts, and behaviors without judgment. By practicing mindfulness and paying attention to the present moment, individuals can develop a deeper understanding of their emotions and how they impact their well-being. Self-awareness also involves reflecting on past experiences and identifying patterns of behavior that may be contributing to emotional distress. By acknowledging and accepting these patterns, individuals can take steps to make positive changes and improve their emotional wellness.

In addition to cultivating self-awareness, managing emotions effectively is another key aspect of promoting emotional wellness. This involves recognizing and understanding one's emotions, and finding healthy ways to express and cope with them. By practicing emotional regulation techniques such as deep breathing, meditation, or journaling, individuals can learn to control their emotional responses and avoid reacting impulsively in challenging situations.

Building emotional resilience through coping strategies can help individuals navigate stress and maintain a sense of balance and well-being.

Furthermore, cultivating positive relationships with others is essential for promoting emotional wellness. Healthy relationships provide support, validation, and a sense of belonging that can contribute to emotional well-being. By fostering open communication, empathy, and trust in their relationships, individuals can create a supportive environment that promotes emotional healing and growth. Connecting with others through social activities, volunteering, or support groups can also help individuals build a sense of community and reduce feelings of isolation or loneliness. By making self-care a priority and seeking support when needed, individuals can create a foundation for long-term emotional well-being and fulfillment.

# Chapter 9: Nurturing Healthy Habits

## - Nutrition and Exercise

Nutrition and exercise are two key components of leading a healthy lifestyle. It is widely recognized that what we eat and how we move our bodies have a significant impact on our overall well-being. When it comes to nutrition, it is important to fuel our bodies with the right balance of nutrients to support our energy levels, immune function, and overall health. This includes consuming a variety of fruits and vegetables, whole grains, lean proteins, and healthy fats. By incorporating these foods into our diet, we can ensure that our bodies are receiving the vitamins, minerals, and antioxidants they need to function optimally.

In addition to eating a balanced diet, regular exercise is essential for maintaining good health. Physical activity has numerous benefits, including improving cardiovascular health, building muscle strength, and boosting mood. Engaging in regular exercise can also help to prevent chronic diseases such as obesity, heart disease, and diabetes. It is recommended that adults aim for at least 150 minutes of moderate-intensity exercise per week, such as brisk walking, cycling, or swimming. Strength training exercises should also be incorporated into a weekly routine to build muscle mass and improve bone density.

When it comes to combining nutrition and exercise, the two work hand in hand to optimize health outcomes. Eating a nutritious diet can help to fuel our workouts and improve our performance, while regular exercise can enhance the absorption of nutrients and promote overall well-being. For example, consuming a post-workout snack or meal that includes a balance of carbohydrates and protein can help to replenish glycogen stores and support muscle repair and growth. Additionally, staying hydrated is essential for both nutrition and exercise, as water plays a crucial role in digestion, nutrient transport, and temperature regulation during physical activity.

One important aspect of nutrition and exercise is finding a balance that works for each individual. It is important to listen to your body's hunger and fullness cues, as well as to pay attention to how different foods and forms of exercise make you feel. Everyone's nutritional needs and fitness goals are unique, so it is important to tailor your diet and exercise routine to suit your personal preferences and lifestyle. Consulting with a registered dietitian and/or personal trainer can also help to provide guidance and support in achieving your health and wellness goals. By prioritizing a balanced diet rich in fruits, vegetables, whole grains, lean proteins, and healthy fats, and incorporating regular physical activity into your routine, you can support your body's health and longevity. Remember to listen to your body, stay hydrated, and seek guidance from healthcare professionals to ensure that you are meeting your individual nutritional and fitness needs. With dedication and consistency, you can achieve optimal health and vitality through the power of nutrition and exercise.

# - Limiting Screen Time

Limiting screen time has become an increasingly important topic of discussion in today's society, as technology becomes more integrated into our daily lives. The excessive use of screens, including smartphones, tablets, computers, and televisions, has been linked to a variety of negative effects on both physical and mental health. While screens can provide valuable information and entertainment, it is important to recognize the potential harm that can come from overuse.

One of the main concerns regarding excessive screen time is its impact on physical health. Prolonged screen use has been associated with a sedentary lifestyle, which can lead to obesity, cardiovascular disease, and other health issues. Additionally, staring at a screen for extended periods of time can cause eye strain, headaches, and even vision problems. It is crucial to take breaks and engage in physical activity to mitigate these risks.

Furthermore, excessive screen time has been shown to have negative effects on mental health. Studies have found a correlation between high screen use and an increased risk of depression, anxiety, and other mental health disorders.

The constant exposure to digital devices can also lead to poor sleep quality, as the blue light emitted by screens can disrupt the body's natural sleep-wake cycle. Limiting screen time, especially before bedtime, can help improve sleep patterns and overall mental well-being.

In addition to its effects on physical and mental health, excessive screen time can also have a detrimental impact on social relationships. Spending too much time on devices can detract from face-to-face interactions with family and friends, leading to feelings of isolation and disconnection. It is important to set boundaries and prioritize in-person communication to foster strong, meaningful relationships.

Parents play a crucial role in setting limits on screen time for their children. The American Academy of Pediatrics recommends that children under the age of 18 months avoid screen time, except for video chatting. For children aged 2 to 5 years, screen time should be limited to one hour per day of high-quality programming. Parents should also model positive behavior by limiting their own screen time and engaging in other activities with their children.

Educators can also play a significant role in promoting healthy screen habits among students. Schools can incorporate lessons on digital citizenship and media literacy to help students understand the benefits and risks of technology. Teachers can also encourage students to engage in hands-on activities and outdoor play to balance their screen time. By being mindful of the potential negative effects of excessive screen use on physical and mental health, as well as social relationships, individuals can take proactive steps to reduce their screen time and engage in more meaningful activities. Parents, educators, and policymakers must work together to promote responsible screen habits and create a healthy digital environment for future generations. By setting clear boundaries and prioritizing real-life connections, we can ensure that technology enhances, rather than detracts from, our overall well-being.

## - Establishing Routines

Establishing routines is an essential aspect of creating structure and organization in our daily lives. Routines help us to establish habits and patterns that promote efficiency, productivity, and overall well-being. By following a set routine, we can reduce stress, increase focus, and improve our overall quality of life.

One of the key benefits of establishing routines is that they help us to manage our time more effectively. Having a set routine allows us to prioritize our tasks and allocate our time wisely. This, in turn, helps us to meet deadlines, avoid procrastination, and accomplish our goals in a timely manner. By following a routine, we can also ensure that we are dedicating enough time to all aspects of our lives, including work, family, and self-care.

Another important benefit of routines is that they help to reduce decision fatigue. When we have a set routine in place, we don't have to spend time and energy thinking about what to do next. This frees up mental space and allows us to focus on more important tasks. By automating certain aspects of our day through routines, we can streamline our workflow and make better use of our cognitive resources.

Routines can also help to improve our mental and physical health. By incorporating activities such as exercise, meditation, and healthy eating into our daily routines, we can promote overall well-being and reduce the risk of illness. Routines can also help us to establish healthy sleep patterns, which are essential for optimal health and functioning. By going to bed and waking up at the same time each day, we can ensure that we are getting enough rest and rejuvenation.

In addition to the practical benefits of routines, they can also have a positive impact on our emotional well-being. Routines provide a sense of stability and predictability in our lives, which can help to reduce feelings of anxiety and uncertainty. By knowing what to expect each day, we can feel more in control of our surroundings and better equipped to handle any challenges that may arise. Routines can also foster a sense of accomplishment and satisfaction, as we see the results of our efforts in the form of completed tasks and goals.

Despite the numerous benefits of routines, establishing and maintaining them can be challenging. It can be difficult to break old habits and create new ones, especially when faced with competing demands and distractions. However, by starting small and building gradually, it is possible to create a routine that works for you. It is important to be flexible and willing to adjust your routine as needed, based on feedback and changing circumstances. By approaching the process of establishing routines with patience and persistence, you can create a framework for success and fulfillment in all areas of your life. Routines help us to manage our time effectively, reduce decision fatigue, improve our health and well-being, and enhance our emotional stability. By committing to a set routine and staying consistent, we can create a sense of order and structure in our lives that promotes productivity, happiness, and overall success. By recognizing the importance of routines and making them a priority in our daily lives, we can truly unlock our full potential and live our best lives.

# Chapter 10: Fostering a Positive School Experience

## - Supporting Learning and Academic Success

Supporting learning and academic success is a crucial aspect of education that requires a multifaceted approach to ensure that students reach their fullest potential. In today's rapidly evolving world, the ability to learn and adapt is more important than ever before. As educators, it is our responsibility to provide students with the tools and resources they need to succeed academically and in life. This includes creating a supportive and inclusive learning environment, offering personalized learning opportunities, and fostering a growth mindset in our students.

One of the key components of supporting learning and academic success is creating an inclusive and supportive learning environment. This means creating a safe and welcoming space where all students feel valued and respected. By promoting diversity and inclusion in the classroom, we can help students feel more comfortable taking risks and exploring new ideas. Additionally, providing students with opportunities to collaborate with their peers and engage in meaningful discussions can help foster a sense of community and belonging. When students feel supported and included, they are more likely to be engaged in their learning and perform better academically.

In addition to creating a supportive learning environment, it is important to offer personalized learning opportunities to meet the diverse needs of students. Every student is unique and has different learning styles, interests, and abilities. By providing students with choices and options in how they learn and demonstrate their knowledge, we can help them thrive academically. This may include offering different learning resources, allowing for project-based assessments, and providing opportunities for students to pursue their interests and passions. By tailoring our instruction to meet the individual needs of students, we can help them achieve academic success and reach their full potential.

Furthermore, fostering a growth mindset in our students is essential for supporting learning and academic success. A growth mindset is the belief that intelligence and abilities can be developed through effort and perseverance. By encouraging students to embrace challenges, learn from failure, and persist in the face of obstacles, we can help them develop a positive attitude towards learning and growth. This can lead to increased motivation, improved academic performance, and a lifelong love of learning. As educators, it is important to praise students for their effort and persistence rather than their innate abilities, as this can help foster a growth mindset and support academic success. By promoting diversity and inclusion, tailoring our instruction to meet the individual needs of students, and encouraging a growth mindset, we can help students achieve academic success and reach their fullest potential. As educators, it is our responsibility to provide students with the tools and resources they need to succeed academically and in life. By working together to support learning and academic success, we can help students thrive in the classroom and beyond.

## - Building Relationships with Teachers

Building relationships with teachers is an essential aspect of the educational experience for students. Teachers play a crucial role in shaping the academic and personal development of their students. By fostering positive relationships with teachers, students can enhance their learning experience, improve their academic performance, and develop important social and emotional skills. Building relationships with teachers requires mutual respect, effective communication, and a commitment to collaboration.

One of the key factors in building relationships with teachers is showing respect and appreciation for their expertise and dedication. Teachers devote their time and energy to educating students and helping them succeed, so it is important for students to recognize and respect the hard work and dedication that teachers put into their jobs. By showing respect for teachers, students can create a positive and supportive environment in which both parties can work together to achieve academic success. This can be done by actively listening to teachers, following their instructions, and showing gratitude for their efforts.

Effective communication is another important aspect of building relationships with teachers. Communication is essential for establishing and maintaining positive relationships with teachers, as it allows for the exchange of information, feedback, and support. Students should communicate openly and honestly with their teachers, sharing their thoughts, concerns, and progress in class. By engaging in regular communication with teachers, students can build trust and rapport, which can lead to a more productive and successful academic experience. Effective communication also involves demonstrating active listening skills, asking for clarification when needed, and providing feedback in a respectful and constructive manner.

Collaboration is a key component of building relationships with teachers. Collaboration involves working together with teachers to set goals, solve problems, and achieve academic success. By collaborating with teachers, students can take an active role in their education and develop important skills such as critical thinking, problem-solving, and teamwork. Collaboration also fosters a sense of mutual respect and appreciation between students and teachers, as both parties work together towards a common goal. Students can collaborate with teachers by participating in class discussions, seeking feedback on assignments, and asking for assistance when needed. By working collaboratively with teachers, students can build strong and supportive relationships that contribute to their academic success. By showing respect and appreciation for teachers, engaging in effective communication, and working collaboratively to achieve academic success, students can enhance their learning experience and develop important social and emotional skills. Building relationships with teachers is a two-way street that requires effort and commitment from both parties. By investing time and energy into building positive relationships with teachers, students can create a supportive and nurturing environment in which they can thrive academically and personally.

## - Encouraging a Growth Mindset

Encouraging a Growth Mindset

In recent years, the concept of a growth mindset has gained significant attention in the fields of psychology, education, and business. Coined by psychologist Carol Dweck, a growth mindset is the belief that one's abilities and intelligence can be developed through effort, perseverance, and learning. This contrasts with a fixed mindset, where individuals believe that their abilities are static and predetermined. Encouraging a growth mindset in oneself and others has been shown to lead to increased motivation, resilience, and ultimately, success. In this essay, we will explore the principles of a growth mindset, discuss strategies for fostering it, and highlight its benefits in various aspects of life.

One of the key principles of a growth mindset is the understanding that failure is not a permanent state, but rather a valuable learning opportunity. People with a growth mindset view setbacks and challenges as stepping stones to growth and improvement, rather than insurmountable barriers. This perspective allows individuals to embrace challenges, take risks, and persevere in the face of obstacles. By reframing failure as a temporary setback that provides valuable insights and feedback, individuals can cultivate a resilient attitude and develop a willingness to try new approaches and strategies.

Another important aspect of a growth mindset is the belief in the power of effort and practice. People with a growth mindset understand that talent and intelligence are not fixed traits, but rather skills that can be developed through dedication and hard work. This mindset fosters a sense of agency and control over one's development, empowering individuals to take ownership of their learning and growth. By prioritizing effort and perseverance over innate ability, individuals with a growth mindset are more likely to engage in deliberate practice, seek feedback, and continuously improve their skills and knowledge.

In addition to embracing failure and valuing effort, fostering a growth mindset also involves cultivating a love of learning and curiosity. People with a growth mindset are motivated by a desire to expand their knowledge, explore new ideas, and challenge themselves intellectually. This intrinsic motivation fuels their engagement with tasks and activities, leading to greater creativity, innovation, and mastery. By nurturing a curiosity-driven approach to learning, individuals can overcome self-doubt and perfectionism, and develop a sense of purpose and fulfillment.

So how can we encourage a growth mindset in ourselves and others? One effective strategy is to cultivate a culture of praise and feedback that values effort and improvement over innate talent. By praising individuals for their hard work, perseverance, and progress, rather than their intelligence or natural ability, we can reinforce the belief that success is attainable through effort and dedication. Similarly, providing constructive feedback that focuses on specific behaviors and strategies for improvement can help individuals develop a growth-oriented mindset, and motivate them to take action and make positive changes.

Another important way to foster a growth mindset is to encourage a growth-oriented language and mindset. By using phrases such as "I can learn from this" or "I will improve with practice," individuals can shift their focus from fixed limitations to growth possibilities. Encouraging a growth mindset also involves challenging self-limiting beliefs and assumptions, and replacing them with more empowering and adaptive perspectives. By reframing negative self-talk and beliefs, individuals can develop a more positive and resilient mindset that promotes growth and development.

Ultimately, the benefits of encouraging a growth mindset are far-reaching and transformative. Research has shown that individuals with a growth mindset are more likely to set challenging goals, persist in the face of obstacles, and achieve success in various domains of life. In education, students with a growth mindset have been shown to outperform their peers, exhibit greater motivation and engagement, and develop a love of learning that extends beyond the classroom. In business, employees with a growth mindset are more adaptable, innovative, and resilient in the face of change and uncertainty, leading to greater productivity and success. By embracing a growth mindset and fostering it in ourselves and others, we can unlock our full potential, overcome obstacles, and achieve our goals with confidence and resilience.

# Chapter 11: Handling Challenges and Conflict

## - Resolving Sibling Rivalry

Sibling rivalry is a common phenomenon that occurs in many families around the world. It is a natural part of growing up and can be a normal and healthy aspect of sibling relationships. However, when sibling rivalry becomes excessive or harmful, it can cause significant distress for both the children involved and their parents. Therefore, it is important for parents to be equipped with strategies for resolving sibling rivalry in a constructive and positive manner.

One key strategy for resolving sibling rivalry is to foster open communication between siblings. Encouraging siblings to talk openly and honestly with each other about their feelings can help them to understand each other better and work through their conflicts in a constructive way. Parents can facilitate this communication by creating a safe and supportive space for their children to express themselves and actively listening to their concerns without taking sides.

Another important strategy for resolving sibling rivalry is to set clear and consistent boundaries for acceptable behavior. Establishing rules and expectations for how siblings should treat each other can help to prevent conflicts from escalating and can provide a framework for resolving disputes when they do occur. It is important for parents to enforce these boundaries consistently and fairly, so that all family members understand the consequences of their actions and are held accountable for their behavior.

Additionally, parents can help to reduce sibling rivalry by fostering a sense of equality and fairness in the family. It is important for parents to treat their children fairly and avoid playing favorites, as this can cause feelings of jealousy and resentment among siblings. Encouraging siblings to support and encourage each other, rather than compete for attention or praise, can help to build a sense of camaraderie and teamwork within the family.

It is also important for parents to acknowledge and validate their children's feelings when conflicts arise. By empathizing with their children and recognizing their emotions, parents can help siblings to feel understood and supported, which can in turn reduce the intensity of their conflicts. It is important for parents to remain calm and patient when mediating conflicts between siblings, and to avoid taking sides or placing blame on one child over another.

In some cases, siblings may benefit from the involvement of a neutral third party, such as a family therapist or counselor, to help them work through their conflicts. A trained professional can provide an objective perspective on the situation and offer strategies for improving communication and resolving disputes in a healthy and productive way. Family therapy can also help parents to better understand the underlying causes of sibling rivalry and develop more effective strategies for managing conflicts within the family. By taking a proactive and thoughtful approach to resolving conflicts between siblings, parents can help their children to develop healthier and more positive relationships with each other. By promoting empathy, cooperation, and mutual respect within the family, parents can create a more harmonious and supportive environment for all family members to thrive.

# - Addressing Behavioral Issues

Addressing behavioral issues is a critical aspect of creating a positive and productive environment in any setting, whether it be in a school, workplace, or home. Behavioral issues can manifest in a variety of ways, including defiance, aggression, impulsivity, and lack of self-control. These behaviors can not only disrupt the learning or working environment but can also have negative consequences for the individual exhibiting them. Addressing behavioral issues requires a proactive and systematic approach that takes into account the underlying causes of the behavior and utilizes evidence-based strategies to address and modify them.

One of the key principles in addressing behavioral issues is understanding that behavior is a form of communication. When individuals exhibit challenging behaviors, they may be trying to express their needs or emotions in a way that they feel is most effective. By taking the time to understand the root cause of the behavior, whether it be frustration, anxiety, or a need for attention, educators, employers, or parents can begin to address the underlying issues and help the individual develop more adaptive ways of expressing themselves.

In addition to understanding the underlying causes of behavior, it is important to establish clear and consistent expectations and consequences for behavior. This involves setting clear rules and boundaries, as well as regularly reinforcing positive behaviors and providing consequences for negative behaviors. Consistency is key in ensuring that individuals understand what is expected of them and what will happen if they do not meet those expectations. By providing a structured environment with clear guidelines, individuals are more likely to understand the consequences of their actions and make better choices.

Another important aspect of addressing behavioral issues is utilizing evidence-based strategies to support individuals in developing more positive behaviors. This may involve implementing programs that teach social skills, emotional regulation, and problem-solving skills, as well as providing individualized support and interventions for those who need it. These strategies are based on research and have been shown to be effective in helping individuals develop more adaptive behaviors and cope with challenges in a constructive way.

It is also important to involve all relevant stakeholders in the process of addressing behavioral issues. This may include teachers, administrators, parents, and mental health professionals, who can provide valuable insights and support in developing effective strategies for addressing behavior. Collaborating with these stakeholders can help ensure that interventions are comprehensive and tailored to the individual needs of each person, as well as provide a support system for both the individual and those working with them.

In summary, it is important to approach behavioral issues with empathy and understanding. Individuals who exhibit challenging behaviors are often struggling with their own emotions and needs, and it is important to acknowledge and validate these feelings while also providing guidance and support in developing more positive behaviors. By approaching behavioral issues with compassion and empathy, we can create a more supportive and inclusive environment that fosters growth and development for all individuals involved. By understanding the underlying causes of behavior, setting clear expectations and consequences, utilizing evidence-based strategies, involving all stakeholders, and approaching the issue with empathy and understanding, we can create a positive and supportive environment that promotes growth and development for all individuals involved. By working together and supporting each other, we can create a more inclusive and peaceful society where everyone has the opportunity to thrive.

# - Dealing with Teenage Rebellion

Teenage rebellion is a common phase that many adolescents go through during their development. It is a period characterized by defiance, independence, and a desire to challenge authority figures. This rebellion can manifest in various ways, such as breaking rules, experimenting with risky behaviors, or refusing to comply with parental expectations. While teenage rebellion is a natural part of growing up, it can be challenging for parents and caregivers to navigate. In order to effectively deal with teenage rebellion, it is important to understand the underlying causes and adopt a patient and empathetic approach.

One of the key factors contributing to teenage rebellion is the need for autonomy and independence. As adolescents strive to assert their identity and establish their place in the world, they may feel the urge to push back against parental authority. This desire for independence can lead to conflicts with parents, as teenagers seek to set their own rules and boundaries. It is important for parents to recognize and validate their teenager's need for autonomy, while also establishing clear guidelines and expectations. By fostering open communication and negotiating boundaries together, parents can help their teenagers navigate the transition to independence in a healthy way.

Another factor that can contribute to teenage rebellion is peer influence. As adolescents spend more time with their peers and seek acceptance from their social group, they may be swayed by the behaviors and attitudes of their friends.

Peer pressure can lead teenagers to engage in risky behaviors or adopt rebellious attitudes in order to fit in with their peers. To address this, parents can encourage their teenagers to choose friends who have a positive influence and to engage in activities that align with their values and goals. By fostering supportive relationships and promoting healthy peer interactions, parents can help their teenagers resist negative influences and make more positive choices.

In addition to autonomy and peer influence, changes in brain development also play a role in teenage rebellion. The adolescent brain undergoes significant changes during this period, particularly in the prefrontal cortex, which is responsible for decision-making, impulse control, and emotional regulation. These changes can lead to increased risk-taking behavior, impulsivity, and emotional volatility in teenagers. Understanding the neurobiological basis of teenage rebellion can help parents approach their teenagers with empathy and patience, recognizing that their behaviors are influenced by biological factors beyond their control.

When faced with teenage rebellion, it is important for parents to approach the situation with empathy, patience, and understanding. It can be easy to react with frustration or anger when faced with defiance or disobedience, but responding in a calm and collected manner can help de-escalate conflicts and foster better communication. By listening to their teenager's perspective, validating their feelings, and offering support and guidance, parents can create a more positive and open relationship with their teenager. This can help build trust and mutual respect, making it easier to navigate the challenges of teenage rebellion together.

In addition to fostering open communication and understanding, setting boundaries and consequences is also important when dealing with teenage rebellion. Establishing clear expectations and consequences for behavior helps teenagers understand the boundaries of acceptable conduct and the consequences of breaking rules. It is important for parents to be consistent in enforcing these boundaries and consequences, while also being flexible and willing to negotiate when necessary. By setting fair and reasonable expectations, parents can help their teenagers learn accountability and responsibility for their actions, while also promoting positive behavior and decision-making.

In some cases, teenage rebellion may be a sign of underlying issues such as mental health problems, substance abuse, or family conflict. It is important for parents to pay attention to warning signs such as sudden changes in behavior, withdrawal from activities, or academic decline. If parents suspect that their teenager may be struggling with more serious issues, it is important to seek professional help from a therapist, counselor, or mental health provider. These professionals can provide the necessary support and guidance to help teenagers address their issues and develop healthy coping strategies. By addressing underlying issues and seeking appropriate treatment, parents can help their teenagers overcome challenges and navigate the complexities of adolescence more effectively. By understanding the underlying causes of rebellion, fostering open communication and empathy, setting clear boundaries and consequences, and seeking professional help when needed, parents can effectively navigate this phase of their teenager's development. By approaching teenage rebellion with patience, understanding, and support, parents can help their teenagers navigate the challenges of adolescence and emerge as confident, responsible, and well-adjusted adults.

# Chapter 12: Promoting Diversity and Inclusivity

## - Teaching Empathy and Respect

Empathy and respect are two essential components of building positive and healthy relationships with others. In the realm of education, teaching empathy and respect is crucial for creating a positive and inclusive learning environment where all students feel valued and heard. Empathy is the ability to understand and share the feelings of another person, while respect is the recognition of the worth and value of others. By incorporating lessons and activities that promote empathy and respect, educators can help students develop important social and emotional skills that will serve them well both inside and outside the classroom.

One of the key ways to teach empathy and respect in the classroom is through modeling positive behavior. Teachers can set a positive example for their students by showing empathy and respect towards each other, as well as towards the students themselves. This includes actively listening to students, acknowledging their feelings, and treating them with kindness and understanding. By modeling these behaviors, teachers can create a safe and supportive classroom environment where students feel encouraged to practice empathy and respect towards their peers.

In addition to modeling positive behavior, educators can also incorporate specific lessons and activities that focus on empathy and respect. For example, teachers can use literature and stories to help students understand different perspectives and experiences. By reading books and discussing characters' feelings and motivations, students can develop a greater sense of empathy towards others. Similarly, teachers can use role-playing activities to help students practice respectful communication and conflict resolution skills. By giving students the opportunity to step into someone else's shoes and consider different viewpoints, educators can help them develop a deeper understanding of empathy and respect.

Furthermore, educators can promote empathy and respect in the classroom by emphasizing the importance of diversity and inclusion. By celebrating students' unique backgrounds, experiences, and perspectives, teachers can create a space where all students feel valued and respected. This can be done through multicultural lessons, guest speakers, and classroom discussions that highlight the importance of respecting and valuing differences. By fostering a culture of inclusivity and acceptance, educators can help students develop a strong sense of empathy towards others who may be different from them.

Another important aspect of teaching empathy and respect is fostering strong relationships between students and educators. By building trusting and supportive relationships with their students, teachers can create a sense of community and belonging in the classroom. This can be achieved through open communication, active listening, and a genuine interest in students' well-being. By creating a positive and caring classroom environment, educators can help students feel valued and respected, which in turn promotes empathy and respect towards others. By modeling positive behavior, incorporating specific lessons and activities, promoting diversity and inclusion, and fostering strong relationships, educators can help students develop important social and emotional skills that will serve them well in all aspects of their lives. By teaching empathy and respect, educators can help students become empathetic and respectful individuals who can make a positive impact on the world around them.

# - Celebrating Differences

Celebrating differences is an essential aspect of building a diverse and inclusive society. It involves recognizing and appreciating the unique qualities, perspectives, and experiences that individuals from various backgrounds bring to the table. By embracing diversity, we can foster a sense of belonging and understanding among all members of our communities. This not only enriches our social interactions but also contributes to the growth and development of our institutions and organizations.

One of the key benefits of celebrating differences is the opportunity to learn from others. Each individual carries with them a wealth of knowledge and experiences that can offer new insights and perspectives on various issues. By engaging with people who have different backgrounds, beliefs, and worldviews, we can broaden our horizons and challenge our own assumptions. This exchange of ideas can lead to greater creativity, innovation, and problem-solving capabilities within our communities.

Furthermore, celebrating differences helps to create a sense of unity and cohesion among diverse groups of people. When individuals feel accepted and valued for who they are, regardless of their differences, they are more likely to come together and work towards a common goal. This sense of unity can foster a greater sense of community spirit and cooperation, leading to stronger relationships and social connections. By recognizing and celebrating the unique contributions of each individual, we can build a more inclusive and harmonious society.

Another important aspect of celebrating differences is the promotion of equality and social justice. Embracing diversity means acknowledging the disparities and inequalities that exist within our society and working towards addressing them. By celebrating differences, we can challenge prejudice, discrimination, and stigmatization that may arise from ignorance or fear of the unknown. This can help to create a more just and equitable society where all individuals have the opportunity to thrive and succeed, regardless of their background or identity.

In addition to promoting understanding and unity, celebrating differences can also enhance individual growth and personal development. When we are exposed to new ideas, perspectives, and experiences, we have the opportunity to expand our own horizons and challenge our own beliefs. This process of self-reflection and introspection can lead to greater self-awareness and empathy towards others. By embracing diversity, we can become more compassionate, open-minded, and accepting individuals who are better equipped to navigate the complexities of a diverse and interconnected world. By recognizing and valuing the unique qualities and experiences of individuals from diverse backgrounds, we can create a more inclusive, equitable, and cohesive society. Embracing diversity is not just a moral imperative but also a strategic advantage that can lead to greater creativity, innovation, and success in all aspects of our lives. Let us continue to celebrate our differences and build a more harmonious and interconnected world for future generations to come.

# - Creating a Safe Space for Expression

Creating a safe space for expression is essential in fostering an environment where individuals feel comfortable sharing their thoughts, feelings, and opinions without fear of judgment or reprisal. This is particularly important in academic and professional settings where diverse perspectives and ideas are valued. By establishing a safe space, organizations, institutions, and communities can encourage open dialogue, collaboration, and innovation.

One of the key components of creating a safe space for expression is building trust among individuals. Trust is the foundation upon which meaningful communication and engagement can take place. When individuals trust that their views will be respected and heard, they are more likely to speak up and share their perspectives. Trust is built through consistent and honest communication, active listening, and demonstrating empathy and understanding towards others. Organizations can facilitate trust-building by fostering a culture of openness and transparency, and by encouraging feedback and dialogue.

Another important aspect of creating a safe space for expression is promoting inclusivity and diversity. Inclusivity involves recognizing and embracing the unique perspectives, experiences, and backgrounds of individuals, and ensuring that all voices are heard and valued. By promoting inclusivity, organizations can create a culture of respect and acceptance, where individuals feel free to express themselves authentically and contribute their ideas without fear of discrimination or marginalization. Diversity of thought is essential in driving innovation and problem-solving, and by creating a safe space for expression, organizations can tap into the full potential of their teams and unlock new possibilities.

In order to create a safe space for expression, it is important to establish clear guidelines and norms for communication. This includes setting expectations for respectful and constructive dialogue, as well as creating mechanisms for addressing conflicts and disagreements in a productive manner. Organizations can develop codes of conduct, communication guidelines, or conflict resolution processes to help guide interactions and ensure that all individuals feel comfortable participating in discussions. By setting clear boundaries and expectations, organizations can create a sense of safety and security that encourages open and honest expression.

In addition to establishing guidelines for communication, organizations can also provide training and resources to help individuals develop effective communication skills and navigate difficult conversations. This may include workshops on active listening, empathy, conflict resolution, or cultural competence, as well as resources for addressing bias, discrimination, and unconscious stereotypes. By equipping individuals with the tools and knowledge to communicate effectively and respectfully, organizations can promote a culture of understanding and collaboration that values diversity and fosters inclusivity.

Creating a safe space for expression also involves cultivating a culture of feedback and learning. This means creating opportunities for individuals to provide input, share feedback, and reflect on their experiences in a supportive and non-judgmental environment. By encouraging a culture of continuous learning and growth, organizations can foster a sense of openness and vulnerability that allows individuals to express themselves authentically and take risks in sharing their ideas. By promoting a growth mindset and a willingness to learn from mistakes and failures, organizations can create a culture of resilience and adaptability that values innovation and creativity.

Ultimately, creating a safe space for expression is an ongoing process that requires commitment, effort, and collaboration from all individuals involved. By building trust, promoting inclusivity, establishing clear communication guidelines, providing training and resources, and fostering a culture of feedback and learning, organizations can create an environment where individuals feel valued, respected, and empowered to express themselves authentically and contribute their unique perspectives to the conversation. By embracing diversity of thought and promoting open and honest dialogue, organizations can unlock the full potential of their teams, drive innovation and creativity, and create a positive and inclusive culture where all voices are heard and valued.

# Chapter 13: Setting Family Goals and Values

## - Establishing Family Traditions

Family traditions are an important aspect of family life that can create lasting memories and strengthen the bond between family members. These traditions can provide a sense of continuity and stability, especially during times of change or uncertainty. In this discussion, we will explore the benefits of establishing family traditions, as well as practical tips for creating and maintaining these traditions.

One of the key benefits of family traditions is that they can help to create a sense of belonging and connectedness within the family unit. Traditions can also provide a sense of comfort and familiarity, especially for children who thrive on routine and predictability. Knowing that certain traditions will be carried out year after year can create a sense of security and stability for children, helping them to feel grounded and supported within the family structure.

Family traditions can also provide an opportunity for family members to spend quality time together and create cherished memories. Whether it's a weekly game night, an annual holiday celebration, or a special family vacation, these shared experiences can create lasting bonds and build strong relationships between family members. Traditions can also serve as a way to pass down family values and beliefs from one generation to the next. By engaging in traditions that have been passed down through the family, children can learn about their family's history and cultural heritage, helping them to develop a sense of pride and connection to their roots.

When it comes to establishing family traditions, there are a few key factors to consider to ensure that these traditions are meaningful and sustainable. First and foremost, it's important to involve all members of the family in the process of creating and maintaining traditions. This can help to ensure that everyone feels invested in the tradition and that it reflects the values and interests of the entire family. It's also important to be flexible and open to change when it comes to traditions, as family dynamics and interests may evolve over time. Being willing to adapt and modify traditions as needed can help to ensure that they remain relevant and enjoyable for all family members.

Another important aspect of establishing family traditions is consistency. In order for traditions to be meaningful and impactful, they need to be carried out consistently and regularly. This can help to create a sense of anticipation and excitement around the tradition, as well as provide a sense of structure and routine for family members. Consistency can also help to reinforce the importance of the tradition and its significance within the family unit. By making a commitment to uphold and maintain traditions, families can ensure that these rituals will continue to bring joy and meaning to their lives for years to come.

In addition to consistency, it's also important to be creative and innovative when it comes to creating family traditions. Traditions don't have to be elaborate or expensive in order to be meaningful – they can be as simple as a weekly movie night or a monthly hike in the woods. The key is to find activities that resonate with the interests and values of your family and that can be enjoyed by all members. By thinking outside the box and being open to new ideas, families can create traditions that are unique and special to their own family unit. These traditions can provide a sense of belonging and connectedness, create lasting memories and experiences, and help to pass down family values and heritage from one generation to the next. By involving all family members in the process of creating and maintaining traditions, being consistent and flexible, and being creative and innovative, families can establish traditions that will bring joy and meaning to their lives for years to come. So, why not start creating your own family traditions today.

## - Developing a Shared Vision

Developing a shared vision is a crucial aspect of successful leadership and organizational development. A shared vision is a collective understanding of where an organization is heading and what it aims to achieve in the future. It provides a common purpose and direction for all members of the organization, aligning their efforts towards a common goal. Developing a shared vision involves a collaborative process of engaging stakeholders, exploring values and beliefs, and creating a compelling and inspiring picture of the future.

One key step in developing a shared vision is to engage stakeholders at all levels of the organization. This includes employees, managers, and other key stakeholders who have a vested interest in the organization's success. By involving a diverse range of perspectives and insights, organizations can ensure that their shared vision reflects a broad understanding of the organization's purpose and goals. This collaborative approach can help to build buy-in and commitment from all members of the organization, fostering a sense of ownership and accountability for the shared vision.

Another important aspect of developing a shared vision is the exploration of values and beliefs. Organizations must identify and clarify their core values and beliefs, as these will form the foundation of their shared vision. By understanding what is truly important to the organization and its members, leaders can create a vision that resonates with their values and inspires them to work towards a common goal. This process may involve conducting surveys, focus groups, or workshops to gather insights and input from stakeholders, helping to ensure that the shared vision is meaningful and relevant to all members of the organization.

Creating a compelling and inspiring picture of the future is essential in developing a shared vision that motivates and energizes members of the organization. The shared vision should be bold, aspirational, and achievable, inspiring individuals to strive for excellence and work towards a common goal. Leaders must craft a vision that is clear, concise, and easy to communicate, ensuring that all members of the organization can understand and align with its purpose and goals. By painting a compelling picture of the future, leaders can ignite passion and enthusiasm among stakeholders, driving them to collaborate and innovate in pursuit of the shared vision. By engaging stakeholders, exploring values and beliefs, and creating a compelling and inspiring picture of the future, leaders can bring people together towards a common goal. A shared vision provides a clear direction and purpose for the organization, aligning efforts and fostering collaboration among members. By developing a shared vision that is meaningful, relevant, and inspiring, organizations can build a strong foundation for growth, innovation, and success in the future.

# - Aligning Values with Parenting Practices

Aligning values with parenting practices is essential for creating a harmonious and nurturing environment for children to thrive. Parents play a critical role in shaping the beliefs, attitudes, and behaviors of their children through their words and actions. By aligning their values with their parenting practices, parents can effectively model the behavior they want to instill in their children and help them develop a strong moral compass.

One of the key steps in aligning values with parenting practices is for parents to reflect on their own values and beliefs. This requires self-awareness and introspection to identify what is truly important to them and how they want to raise their children. By understanding their own values, parents can ensure that their parenting practices are consistent with their beliefs and principles. This process can involve examining cultural, religious, and personal values to determine how they can be integrated into parenting strategies.

Once parents have identified their values, they can begin to incorporate them into their parenting practices. This may involve setting clear expectations and boundaries for their children based on their values, such as emphasizing the importance of honesty, respect, and empathy. By consistently reinforcing these values through their interactions with their children, parents can help instill these principles in their children's worldview.

Another important aspect of aligning values with parenting practices is the concept of leading by example. Children learn by observing the behavior of their parents, so it is crucial for parents to model the values they want to instill in their children. This means demonstrating respect, kindness, and integrity in their own actions and interactions, as children are more likely to internalize these values when they see them being practiced consistently by their parents.

In addition to modeling values, parents can also engage their children in discussions about values and ethics. This can involve talking about the reasons behind certain rules and expectations, as well as discussing real-life examples of how values are applied in different situations. By involving their children in these conversations, parents can help them understand the rationale behind their values and encourage them to develop their own sense of right and wrong.

It is important for parents to recognize that aligning values with parenting practices is an ongoing process that requires constant reflection and adjustment. As children grow and develop, parents may need to adapt their parenting strategies to meet their changing needs and circumstances. This may involve revisiting their values and beliefs to ensure they are still relevant and meaningful in the context of their children's lives. By reflecting on their own values, modeling behavior, engaging in discussions, and adapting their strategies, parents can create a nurturing environment where their children can learn and grow. Ultimately, aligning values with parenting practices is a powerful way for parents to instill a strong moral foundation in their children and help them become responsible, ethical, and compassionate individuals.

# Chapter 14: Strengthening the Parenting Partnership

## - Communication with Co-Parent

Effective communication with a co-parent is essential for maintaining a healthy and harmonious co-parenting relationship. Co-parenting is a collaborative effort that requires both parents to work together to raise their children successfully, even if they are no longer in a romantic relationship. Communication plays a critical role in co-parenting as it allows parents to make decisions regarding the upbringing of their children, coordinate schedules, and resolve conflicts amicably. However, communicating with a co-parent can sometimes be challenging due to past conflicts, differences in parenting styles, or emotional baggage from the breakup. In this essay, we will explore strategies for improving communication with a co-parent and fostering a positive co-parenting relationship.

One of the key components of effective communication with a co-parent is setting clear boundaries and expectations. Establishing boundaries helps to create a respectful and productive communication dynamic between co-parents. Boundaries can include guidelines for how and when to communicate, the topics that are off-limits, and the tone and language to use in conversations. By setting clear boundaries, co-parents can avoid misunderstandings, reduce conflict, and create a sense of predictability in their communication. It is essential for co-parents to discuss and agree upon these boundaries together to ensure that both parties are on the same page.

Another important aspect of effective communication with a co-parent is active listening. Active listening involves fully concentrating on what the other person is saying, understanding their message, and responding appropriately. Co-parents should make a conscious effort to listen to each other without interrupting, making assumptions, or jumping to s. Active listening helps to foster empathy, understanding, and collaboration between co-parents, leading to more constructive conversations and better outcomes for the children. By practicing active listening, co-parents can build trust, reduce conflicts, and strengthen their co-parenting relationship.

In addition to active listening, validation is a powerful communication tool that can improve the quality of conversations between co-parents. Validation involves acknowledging the other person's feelings, experiences, and perspectives without judgment or criticism. When co-parents validate each other's emotions and viewpoints, it creates a sense of respect, empathy, and validation, which can lead to greater understanding and cooperation. Validation can help to de-escalate conflicts, build rapport, and foster a more positive and supportive co-parenting relationship. By validating each other, co-parents can demonstrate empathy, build trust, and create a safe space for open and honest communication.

Furthermore, practicing effective communication skills such as assertiveness, empathy, and conflict resolution can enhance the quality of communication between co-parents. Assertiveness involves expressing your thoughts and feelings honestly and respectfully without being aggressive or passive. Co-parents should feel empowered to communicate their needs, concerns, and boundaries assertively, while also listening to and respecting the other person's perspective. Empathy involves understanding and sharing the other person's feelings, which can help to build trust, connection, and collaboration between co-parents. By practicing empathy, co-parents can validate each other's emotions, demonstrate understanding, and foster a sense of mutual respect. Conflict resolution involves addressing disagreements, finding common ground, and working together to find solutions that benefit the children. Co-parents should approach conflicts with a problem-solving mindset, focusing on the interests of the children and seeking win-win solutions that address both parties' needs and concerns. By using effective communication skills, co-parents can navigate conflicts, build rapport, and strengthen their co-parenting relationship. Setting clear boundaries, practicing active listening, validation, and using effective communication skills such as assertiveness, empathy, and conflict resolution can help co-parents improve the quality of their communication and create a more positive co-parenting dynamic. By working together to enhance their communication skills, co-parents can build trust, reduce conflicts, and promote the well-being of their children. Ultimately, effective communication is the key to successful co-parenting and ensuring that children thrive in a supportive and nurturing co-parenting environment.

# - Sharing Responsibilities

Sharing responsibilities is a vital component of any successful organization or team. By distributing tasks and duties among members, it not only lightens the workload for individuals but also ensures that all aspects of a project or goal are covered and completed efficiently. It fosters a sense of collaboration and cooperation among team members, leading to increased productivity and satisfaction. When responsibilities are shared, each member feels valued and important, knowing that their contributions are essential to the overall success of the team.

One of the key benefits of sharing responsibilities is the ability to leverage the strengths and skills of each team member. When tasks are assigned based on individual strengths, it results in higher quality work and better outcomes. For example, if one team member excels at data analysis while another is a strong communicator, assigning tasks that align with their strengths will lead to a more comprehensive and effective result. By sharing responsibilities in this way, teams can leverage the diverse skill sets of their members to achieve their goals more efficiently.

In addition to harnessing individual strengths, sharing responsibilities also promotes a sense of accountability within the team. When tasks are clearly assigned and each team member knows their role and responsibilities, it creates a structure that holds everyone accountable for their contributions. This accountability fosters a sense of ownership and commitment to the team's success, as each member is aware of the impact of their work on the overall outcome. When responsibilities are shared in a transparent and equitable manner, it builds trust among team members and creates a culture of accountability and mutual respect.

Furthermore, sharing responsibilities can help distribute the workload more evenly among team members, preventing burnout and overburdening individuals. When tasks are shared, it allows for a more balanced distribution of work, ensuring that no one person is carrying the majority of the load. This not only prevents individual team members from becoming overwhelmed but also promotes a healthier work-life balance for everyone involved. By sharing responsibilities and workload, teams can ensure that all members are contributing equally and that the workload is distributed in a fair and sustainable way.

Another important aspect of sharing responsibilities is the opportunity it provides for skill development and growth. When team members are given the chance to take on new responsibilities and tasks, it allows them to expand their skill sets and knowledge base. This not only benefits the individual team member but also strengthens the team as a whole, as it increases the overall capabilities and expertise of the group. By encouraging team members to take on new challenges and learn new skills, sharing responsibilities promotes a culture of continuous learning and improvement within the team. By distributing tasks and duties among team members, it leverages individual strengths, promotes accountability, prevents burnout, and fosters skill development and growth. When responsibilities are shared in a transparent and equitable manner, it creates a culture of collaboration, cooperation, and mutual respect within the team. Ultimately, sharing responsibilities leads to increased productivity, quality of work, and overall success for the team. It is essential for any organization or team looking to achieve their goals and objectives in a sustainable and efficient manner.

## - Resolving Disagreements

Resolving disagreements is a critical aspect of interpersonal relationships, both in professional and personal settings. Disagreements can arise due to differences in opinions, values, beliefs, or perspectives. It is important to address and resolve these disagreements effectively in order to maintain positive relationships and cultivate a healthy environment for communication and collaboration.

One of the key steps in resolving disagreements is to understand the root cause of the disagreement. This involves actively listening to the other party's perspective and empathizing with their point of view. By understanding the underlying reasons for the disagreement, you can work towards finding a mutually acceptable solution that addresses the concerns of both parties.

Communication plays a crucial role in resolving disagreements. Effective communication involves expressing your thoughts and feelings clearly and respectfully, as well as actively listening to the other party. It is important to avoid making assumptions or jumping to s, and instead, focus on understanding the other person's perspective and finding common ground. Open and honest communication can help clarify misunderstandings and facilitate a constructive dialogue towards finding a resolution.

Another important aspect of resolving disagreements is maintaining a positive and respectful attitude. It is important to approach the situation with an open mind and a willingness to compromise. By showing respect for the other party and their perspective, you can create a more collaborative and constructive environment for resolving the disagreement. Avoiding negative behaviors such as blaming, criticizing, or attacking the other person can help de-escalate the conflict and foster a more productive conversation.

In some cases, it may be helpful to seek the assistance of a neutral third party to help mediate the disagreement. A mediator can facilitate communication between the parties, help clarify misunderstandings, and guide the discussion towards finding a mutually acceptable solution. Mediation can be particularly useful in situations where the disagreement is complex or emotionally charged, and where the parties are struggling to find common ground on their own.

When resolving disagreements, it is important to be willing to make compromises and find a solution that is acceptable to all parties involved. This may involve finding a middle ground, exploring alternative solutions, or finding creative ways to address the underlying issues. By working together towards a mutually beneficial solution, you can strengthen the relationship and build trust and understanding between the parties. By approaching disagreements with a positive and respectful attitude, seeking to understand the root causes of the conflict, and being open to compromise, you can navigate through disagreements in a constructive and productive manner. Remember that disagreements are a natural part of any relationship, and by approaching them with patience, empathy, and a focus on finding common ground, you can resolve conflicts and strengthen your relationships in the process.

# Chapter 15: Embracing Change and Adaptability

## - Transitioning through Life Stages

Life is a journey filled with various stages and transitions that shape our identities, relationships, and personal growth. Each phase of life presents its own set of challenges and opportunities, requiring individuals to adapt and navigate their way through change. From infancy to old age, we experience different milestones and transitions that influence our development and well-being. Understanding and effectively managing these life stages can enhance our overall quality of life and contribute to our sense of fulfillment and happiness.

One of the first major life transitions we experience is infancy, which marks the beginning of our journey from dependence to independence. During this stage, infants rely on their caregivers for everything from food and clothing to comfort and security. As they grow and develop, they begin to explore their environment, form attachments with others, and develop basic skills such as walking and talking. This period of rapid physical, cognitive, and emotional growth lays the foundation for future learning and relationships. Parents play a crucial role in supporting their infants through this transition, providing love, nurturing, and guidance to help them thrive and develop a secure sense of self.

The next significant life stage is childhood, which encompasses the period from early childhood to adolescence. This phase is characterized by continued growth and development, as children acquire new skills, knowledge, and social abilities. They begin to form more complex relationships with peers, teachers, and other adults, and start to develop a sense of identity and autonomy. As children transition from elementary school to middle school and high school, they face new challenges such as academic pressures, peer relationships, and personal identity issues. Parents, educators, and other caregivers play a vital role in providing support, guidance, and encouragement to help children navigate through these changes and build resilience and self-confidence.

Adolescence is a critical period of transition marked by physical, emotional, and social changes as individuals navigate the transition from childhood to adulthood. During this stage, teenagers experience significant growth spurts, hormonal changes, and brain development, which can impact their behaviors, emotions, and decision-making abilities. They begin to assert their independence, experiment with new roles and identities, and explore their values, beliefs, and goals. Adolescents also face challenges such as peer pressure, academic stress, and identity formation, which can influence their mental health and well-being. Parents, teachers, and other adults can support teenagers through this phase by providing guidance, resources, and a safe space for them to express their thoughts and feelings.

The transition to adulthood is a major life stage that involves assuming new responsibilities, roles, and challenges as individuals enter the workforce, pursue higher education, and establish their own families. Young adults face a range of decisions and choices related to career paths, relationships, housing, and lifestyle, which can shape their future trajectories and quality of life. They must navigate through financial pressures, societal expectations, and personal aspirations as they transition from dependence on parents to self-sufficiency and independence. Building a strong support network, seeking guidance from mentors, and developing essential life skills such as time management, communication, and problem-solving can help young adults successfully navigate through this stage and achieve their personal and professional goals.

Midlife is another significant life stage that typically occurs in the middle years of adulthood, usually between the ages of 40 and 60. During this phase, individuals often experience a sense of transition, reflection, and reevaluation as they confront existential questions about their identity, values, and purpose in life. They may reassess their career paths, relationships, and personal goals, and make decisions about their future direction and priorities. Midlife can be a time of personal growth, self-discovery, and transformation as individuals explore new opportunities, passions, and relationships. Seeking support from friends, family, therapists, or support groups can help navigate through this stage and embrace the changes and challenges that come with midlife transitions.

Later adulthood, also known as the senior years or elderly stage, is a period marked by physical, cognitive, and emotional changes as individuals transition from midlife to old age. During this stage, older adults may experience declines in health, mobility, and cognitive functioning, which can impact their independence, quality of life, and social interactions. They may face challenges such as retirement, loss of loved ones, financial instability, and changes in living arrangements, which can increase feelings of isolation, loneliness, and depression. Building a strong social support network, engaging in meaningful activities and hobbies, staying physically and mentally active, and seeking professional help when needed are essential strategies for navigating through the challenges and transitions of later adulthood. From infancy to old age, we experience a series of milestones and transitions that require us to adapt, learn, and grow. Understanding the challenges and opportunities presented by each life stage can help us effectively navigate through change and make the most of our experiences. Seeking support from friends, family, mentors, therapists, or support groups can provide guidance, encouragement, and reassurance as we face the transitions and challenges of different life stages. By embracing change, fostering resilience, and cultivating a positive mindset, we can navigate through life transitions with confidence, grace, and resilience.

# - Coping with Family Changes

Family changes are an inevitable part of life that can be both challenging and rewarding. Whether it be the addition of a new family member, a change in family dynamics, or a loss of a loved one, these changes can have a significant impact on individuals and their relationships within the family unit. Coping with family changes requires resilience, communication, and support from one another.

One of the key ways to cope with family changes is through open and honest communication. It is essential to discuss feelings, concerns, and expectations with one another in order to navigate through the changes as a family unit.

Communication can help to address any misunderstandings, resolve conflicts, and build stronger relationships within the family. By fostering a safe and supportive environment for open communication, family members can feel heard and understood as they navigate through the changes together.

Another important aspect of coping with family changes is resilience. Change can be difficult and unpredictable, but having resilience can help individuals and families adapt and bounce back from challenges. Resilience is the ability to cope with stress, adversity, and setbacks in a healthy and positive way. By focusing on one's strengths, maintaining a positive attitude, and seeking support from others, individuals can build resilience and navigate through family changes with greater ease.

Seeking support from one another and external resources can also help families cope with changes. Support from family members, friends, and professionals can provide comfort, guidance, and reassurance during challenging times. It is important for individuals to lean on one another and create a support network that can help them navigate through the changes together. Additionally, seeking help from therapists, counselors, or support groups can provide additional tools and strategies to cope with family changes and build resilience.

Self-care is another important aspect of coping with family changes. Taking care of oneself physically, emotionally, and mentally can help individuals manage stress, maintain balance, and navigate through the changes more effectively. Engaging in activities that bring joy, relaxation, and comfort can help individuals recharge and refocus during challenging times. It is important for individuals to prioritize self-care and make time for themselves amidst the changes in order to maintain their well-being and resilience. By fostering open and honest communication, building resilience, seeking support, and practicing self-care, individuals and families can navigate through changes with greater ease and adaptability. Family changes are a natural part of life, and by working together and supporting one another, families can grow stronger and closer through the challenges and transitions that come their way.

## - Embracing the Unexpected

Embracing the unexpected is a key aspect of both personal growth and professional development. In our ever-changing world, it is important to be open-minded and adaptable in order to navigate the twists and turns that life throws at us. While it may be tempting to resist change and cling to stability, learning to embrace the unexpected can lead to new opportunities and experiences that we may not have considered otherwise.

One of the main reasons why embracing the unexpected is important is that it allows us to break free from our comfort zones and expand our horizons. When we are faced with unexpected challenges or opportunities, we are forced to think outside the box and come up with creative solutions. This can push us to grow in ways that we never thought possible, both personally and professionally. By embracing the unexpected, we can learn to be more flexible and adaptive in our thinking, which can help us to overcome obstacles and achieve our goals.

Another benefit of embracing the unexpected is that it can lead to increased resilience and emotional intelligence. When we are able to roll with the punches and adapt to changing circumstances, we can build up our resilience and ability to bounce back from setbacks. This can help us to navigate the ups and downs of life with grace and poise, and can also improve our ability to manage stress and pressure. Additionally, embracing the unexpected can help us to develop our emotional intelligence, as we learn to recognize and manage our own emotions and the emotions of others in difficult situations.

In a professional context, embracing the unexpected can be especially important. In today's fast-paced and unpredictable business world, companies and individuals need to be able to adapt quickly to changing market conditions and new technologies. Those who are able to embrace the unexpected and think on their feet are more likely to succeed in a competitive marketplace. By being open to new challenges and opportunities, professionals can demonstrate their flexibility and creativity, which can set them apart from their peers.

Embracing the unexpected can also lead to greater innovation and creativity. When we are willing to step outside of our comfort zones and embrace uncertainty, we are more likely to come up with new ideas and solutions. This can be especially valuable in a professional setting, where innovation is often the key to staying ahead of the competition. By embracing the unexpected, we can create a culture of innovation within our organizations, where new ideas are welcomed and encouraged.

To truly embrace the unexpected, it is important to adopt a growth mindset. Rather than seeing unexpected events as threats or obstacles, we should view them as opportunities for learning and growth. By approaching the unexpected with a positive attitude and a willingness to learn, we can turn challenges into opportunities and setbacks into stepping stones towards success. This mindset shift can help us to build resilience, creativity, and adaptability, all of which are essential skills in today's rapidly changing world. By being open-minded and adaptable, we can navigate the challenges and opportunities that come our way with grace and resilience. Embracing the unexpected can lead to increased creativity, innovation, and emotional intelligence, and can help us to thrive in an ever-changing world. By adopting a growth mindset and staying open to new possibilities, we can turn unexpected events into opportunities for learning and growth. So, embrace the unexpected and see where it takes you.

# Chapter 16: Emphasizing the Power of Love and Support

## - Showing Affection and Encouragement

Showing affection and encouragement are essential aspects of human relationships that play a significant role in fostering emotional connections and promoting positive behaviors. Whether in personal relationships, professional settings, or educational environments, expressing affection and encouragement can have a profound impact on individuals' well-being and productivity. By demonstrating care, support, and validation, we can help others feel valued, empowered, and motivated to reach their full potential.

Affection can be expressed in a variety of ways, including through physical gestures, verbal affirmations, and acts of kindness. Hugs, kisses, and gentle touches can convey warmth and closeness, while saying "I love you," "I care about you," or "You mean a lot to me" can reaffirm emotional bonds and deepen connections. Additionally, small acts of kindness, such as giving compliments, sending thoughtful notes, or offering help without being asked, can demonstrate consideration and compassion. By showing affection in these ways, we can create a positive atmosphere of trust and intimacy that encourages open communication and emotional expression.

Encouragement is another important aspect of nurturing relationships and promoting personal growth. By providing support, motivation, and positive reinforcement, we can help individuals overcome challenges, build confidence, and achieve their goals. Encouragement can take many forms, such as praising efforts, providing constructive feedback, offering guidance, and celebrating successes. By acknowledging progress, highlighting strengths, and offering reassurance during setbacks, we can inspire resilience, perseverance, and a positive mindset. Encouragement is like a gentle push that propels individuals forward, instilling belief in themselves and their abilities.

In professional settings, showing affection and encouragement can boost morale, increase job satisfaction, and enhance teamwork. When managers and supervisors express care, appreciation, and recognition towards their employees, they create a supportive work environment where individuals feel valued and motivated to perform at their best. By acknowledging employees' efforts, acknowledging accomplishments, and providing opportunities for growth and development, leaders can foster a culture of respect, trust, and collaboration.

In educational settings, showing affection and encouragement can positively impact students' learning experiences, academic performance, and emotional well-being. Teachers and instructors who express care, support, and encouragement towards their students can create a positive and nurturing classroom environment where students feel safe, respected, and motivated to learn. By providing constructive feedback, offering guidance, and acknowledging students' efforts and achievements, educators can inspire confidence, motivation, and a love for learning. Additionally, showing affection and encouragement can help students build resilience, develop a growth mindset, and foster positive relationships with their peers and teachers. By expressing care, support, and validation towards others, we can create a culture of empathy, trust, and collaboration that fosters mutual respect, understanding, and connection. So let us continue to express our love and support for one another, knowing that a little affection and encouragement can go a long way in creating meaningful and fulfilling relationships.

# - Expressing Gratitude

Expressing gratitude is a fundamental aspect of human interaction that has been studied extensively in the fields of psychology, sociology, and communication. Gratitude is defined as the feeling of thankfulness and appreciation for something received or experienced, and it plays a crucial role in fostering positive relationships and psychological well-being. In recent years, researchers have delved deeper into the effects of expressing gratitude on individuals' mental health, social connections, and overall life satisfaction. This essay will explore the benefits of expressing gratitude, different ways to do so, and its impact on society as a whole.

One of the most significant benefits of expressing gratitude is its positive impact on mental health. Research has shown that individuals who regularly practice gratitude report higher levels of subjective well-being, lower levels of depression and anxiety, and greater overall life satisfaction. By focusing on the positive aspects of their lives and feeling grateful for them, individuals can shift their mindset from one of scarcity to one of abundance. This shift in perspective can lead to increased resilience in the face of adversity and a greater sense of optimism about the future. Additionally, expressing gratitude has been linked to improved self-esteem and a greater capacity for empathy and compassion towards others.

In addition to benefiting mental health, expressing gratitude also plays a crucial role in fostering strong social connections and relationships. When individuals express gratitude towards others, it not only makes the recipient feel valued and appreciated but also strengthens the bond between the two parties. Gratitude serves as a social glue that can enhance trust, loyalty, and mutual respect in interpersonal relationships. Furthermore, individuals who express gratitude are often perceived as more likable, trustworthy, and empathetic, which can lead to greater social support and a sense of belonging. By cultivating a culture of gratitude in their interactions with others, individuals can create a positive feedback loop that promotes healthy relationships and community cohesion.

There are various ways in which individuals can express gratitude in their daily lives, ranging from simple acts of kindness to more formal expressions of appreciation. One of the most straightforward ways to express gratitude is through verbal communication, such as saying "thank you" or expressing appreciation for a specific action or gift. However, gratitude can also be expressed through non-verbal means, such as through gestures, body language, or written notes. Small acts of kindness, such as holding the door open for someone or offering to help with a task, can also serve as expressions of gratitude. Additionally, individuals can practice gratitude through reflective exercises, such as keeping a gratitude journal or engaging in daily mindfulness practices that focus on the positive aspects of their lives.

The impact of expressing gratitude extends beyond individual well-being and interpersonal relationships to society as a whole. Research has shown that communities and organizations that cultivate a culture of gratitude are more resilient, cohesive, and productive. In workplaces, expressing gratitude towards employees can boost morale, increase job satisfaction, and improve overall performance. In schools, promoting gratitude among students can enhance their sense of belonging, motivation, and academic achievement. In communities, fostering a spirit of gratitude can promote social cohesion, empathy, and altruism, leading to a more harmonious and inclusive society. By recognizing and appreciating the contributions of others, individuals can create a positive ripple effect that benefits not only themselves but also their communities and the world at large. By cultivating a mindset of gratitude and practicing it in their daily interactions, individuals can unlock a host of benefits, from improved mental health and social relationships to increased resilience and productivity. Through simple acts of kindness, verbal expressions of appreciation, and reflective practices, individuals can harness the transformative power of gratitude to create a more positive and fulfilling life for themselves and those around them.

## - Building Emotional Connections

Building emotional connections is crucial in both personal and professional relationships. It is important to understand how people connect emotionally, as it can significantly impact the overall success and satisfaction of these relationships. Emotional connections involve establishing a deep and meaningful bond with someone on an emotional level, which goes beyond just surface-level interactions. When individuals feel emotionally connected to one another, they are more likely to trust, support, and empathize with one another, which can lead to stronger and more fulfilling relationships.

One of the key components of building emotional connections is effective communication. Communication plays a crucial role in connecting with others on an emotional level, as it allows individuals to express their thoughts, feelings, and emotions in a clear and open manner. When communication is effective, it helps people feel heard, understood, and valued, which can foster a sense of emotional connection. Active listening is also an important aspect of effective communication when building emotional connections. By actively listening to others, individuals can show empathy, understanding, and support, which can help create a stronger emotional bond.

Another important factor in building emotional connections is showing vulnerability. Being vulnerable allows individuals to let down their guard and share their true thoughts and emotions with others, which can help create a deeper sense of connection. When individuals are open and honest about their feelings and experiences, it can foster a sense of trust and intimacy in the relationship. It is important to create a safe and supportive environment where individuals feel comfortable sharing their vulnerabilities without fear of judgment or rejection. By showing vulnerability, individuals can build a strong emotional connection based on trust and authenticity.

In addition to effective communication and vulnerability, building emotional connections also requires empathy and understanding. Empathy involves the ability to understand and share the feelings of others, which can help create a deeper sense of connection and compassion. When individuals empathize with one another, they can relate to each other's emotions and experiences, which can foster a stronger bond. It is important to be empathetic and understanding towards others, as it demonstrates care, respect, and consideration for their feelings. By showing empathy, individuals can build emotional connections based on mutual understanding and support.

Furthermore, building emotional connections requires time, effort, and patience. Strong emotional connections do not happen overnight and require a consistent and ongoing effort to maintain and strengthen the relationship. It is important to invest time and energy into building emotional connections with others, as it can lead to more fulfilling and satisfying relationships. Individuals should be patient and understanding as they work towards building emotional connections, as it may take time to develop trust, intimacy, and empathy in the relationship. By investing in the relationship and nurturing it over time, individuals can create a strong emotional connection that is built on mutual trust, respect, and understanding. Effective communication, vulnerability, empathy, and patience are key factors in building emotional connections with others. By fostering a deeper sense of emotional connection, individuals can create meaningful and lasting relationships based on trust, respect, and understanding. It is important to invest time and effort into building emotional connections with others, as it can lead to more satisfying and rewarding relationships in both personal and professional settings. By understanding the importance of emotional connections and actively working towards building them, individuals can create stronger and more meaningful relationships that enrich their lives.

# Chapter 17: Fostering Resilience and Confidence

## - Teaching Problem-Solving Skills

Problem-solving skills are crucial for success in both academic and professional settings. These skills involve the ability to identify a problem, generate possible solutions, evaluate those solutions, and choose the most effective one. By teaching problem-solving skills, educators can help students develop the critical thinking, creativity, and resilience necessary to navigate the challenges they will encounter throughout their lives.

One key aspect of teaching problem-solving skills is fostering a growth mindset in students. A growth mindset is the belief that intelligence and abilities can be developed through effort and practice. By promoting a growth mindset in the classroom, educators can help students see challenges as opportunities for growth rather than obstacles to their success. This mindset encourages students to embrace failure as a natural part of the learning process and to persevere in the face of setbacks.

Another important aspect of teaching problem-solving skills is providing students with opportunities to practice and apply these skills in real-world contexts. This can include engaging students in hands-on, project-based learning experiences that require them to identify problems, develop solutions, and implement those solutions. By integrating problem-solving activities into the curriculum, educators can help students see the relevance of these skills in their everyday lives and future careers.

In addition to hands-on learning experiences, educators can also teach problem-solving skills through explicit instruction. This can involve breaking down the problem-solving process into smaller steps, providing students with strategies and techniques for approaching different types of problems, and modeling problem-solving behavior. By explicitly teaching problem-solving skills, educators can help students develop a toolkit of problem-solving strategies that they can apply in a variety of situations.

Furthermore, educators can incorporate collaborative learning experiences into their teaching to help students develop their problem-solving skills. Collaboration allows students to work together to identify problems, generate ideas, and evaluate solutions. By working in groups, students can benefit from different perspectives and approaches to problem-solving, leading to more innovative and effective solutions. Collaborative learning also helps students develop important communication and teamwork skills that are essential for success in the workplace. By fostering a growth mindset, providing hands-on learning experiences, offering explicit instruction, and promoting collaborative learning, educators can help students develop the critical thinking, creativity, and resilience needed to navigate the challenges they will face throughout their lives. By equipping students with these skills, educators can empower them to confidently tackle problems, make informed decisions, and achieve their goals.

# - Building Self-Esteem

Self-esteem refers to the overall sense of worth and value that an individual has about themselves. It is a crucial element in psychological well-being and plays a significant role in shaping a person's thoughts, feelings, and behaviors. Building self-esteem is a complex process that involves understanding one's strengths and weaknesses, challenging negative beliefs and perceptions, and developing self-compassion. It is essential for individuals to have a healthy level of self-esteem to navigate the challenges of life effectively and maintain a positive sense of self.

One of the key aspects of building self-esteem is to identify and challenge negative beliefs and perceptions about oneself. Many individuals have self-limiting beliefs that hold them back from reaching their full potential and lead to low self-esteem. These beliefs are often ingrained from childhood experiences, societal expectations, or past failures. By identifying these negative beliefs and reframing them in a more positive light, individuals can begin to build a more positive self-image and enhance their self-esteem. For example, instead of thinking "I'm not good enough," one can reframe it as "I am capable of achieving my goals with hard work and perseverance. "

Another important aspect of building self-esteem is to cultivate self-compassion. Self-compassion involves treating oneself with kindness and understanding, especially during times of failure or setbacks. It is important for individuals to recognize that everyone makes mistakes and experiences challenges, and that it is okay to be imperfect. By practicing self-compassion, individuals can develop a greater sense of self-acceptance and self-love, which are essential for building healthy self-esteem. This can involve engaging in self-care activities, such as meditation, exercise, or spending time with loved ones, that help nurture a positive relationship with oneself.

Additionally, developing a sense of self-worth and value is crucial for building self-esteem. This involves recognizing one's unique qualities, strengths, and achievements, and acknowledging their worthiness as an individual. By focusing on their positive attributes and accomplishments, individuals can boost their self-esteem and develop a stronger sense of self-confidence. It is important for individuals to celebrate their successes, no matter how small, and to acknowledge their progress on their journey towards self-improvement. This can involve setting realistic goals, taking steps to achieve them, and celebrating one's achievements along the way. It is essential for individuals to have a healthy level of self-esteem to navigate the challenges of life effectively and maintain a positive sense of self. By practicing self-compassion, reframing negative beliefs, and celebrating one's strengths and achievements, individuals can enhance their self-esteem and develop a greater sense of self-confidence and self-worth. Ultimately, building self-esteem is a journey of self-discovery and self-acceptance that can lead to greater happiness and well-being.

## - Encouraging Perseverance

Perseverance is a key quality that can greatly benefit individuals in their personal and professional lives. It is the ability to persist and push through challenges, setbacks, and obstacles in order to achieve one's goals. Encouraging perseverance in ourselves and others is crucial for personal growth, achievement, and success.

One way to encourage perseverance is to set clear and achievable goals. When individuals have a clear vision of what they want to achieve, they are more likely to stay motivated and focused on their objectives. Setting realistic goals that are attainable but challenging can help individuals see the progress they are making and stay committed to their efforts. By breaking down larger goals into smaller, more manageable tasks, individuals can track their progress and stay on course despite any obstacles they may encounter.

Another important factor in encouraging perseverance is cultivating a positive mindset. Maintaining a positive attitude can help individuals navigate challenges and setbacks with resilience and determination. By viewing obstacles as opportunities for growth and learning, individuals can stay motivated and focused on their goals. It is important to practice self-compassion and self-care during difficult times in order to maintain a positive outlook and keep pushing forward.

Supportive relationships and a strong support system are also essential in encouraging perseverance. Surrounding oneself with people who believe in their abilities and support their goals can provide individuals with the encouragement and motivation they need to persevere. Seeking out mentors, coaches, or peers who can offer guidance, advice, and encouragement can help individuals stay motivated and overcome any obstacles they may face. Building a strong support network can provide individuals with the resources and encouragement they need to persevere through challenges and achieve their goals.

Developing resilience is another important factor in encouraging perseverance. Resilience is the ability to bounce back from setbacks, adapt to change, and overcome adversity. By developing resilience, individuals can strengthen their ability to persevere through challenges and setbacks. Practicing resilience-building activities such as mindfulness, meditation, exercise, and journaling can help individuals build their emotional strength and cope with stress in a healthy way. By developing resilience, individuals can stay focused and motivated in the face of obstacles and setbacks. By setting clear goals, maintaining a positive mindset, building a support system, and developing resilience, individuals can strengthen their ability to persevere through challenges and obstacles. With determination, resilience, and support, individuals can achieve their goals and reach their full potential. Encouraging perseverance in ourselves and others is a valuable investment in personal growth and achievement.

# Chapter 18: Strengthening Family Bonds

## - Spending Quality Time Together

Spending quality time together is essential for building and maintaining healthy relationships. Whether it be with a romantic partner, family members, or friends, investing time in meaningful interactions can strengthen bonds and create lasting memories. Quality time can take many forms, such as engaging in shared activities, having meaningful conversations, or simply being present with one another. It is not just about quantity but also about the depth of connection and intentionality in the time spent together.

One of the key benefits of spending quality time together is the opportunity to truly connect and communicate with one another. In today's fast-paced world, it can be easy to get caught up in our busy schedules and neglect the important relationships in our lives. By setting aside dedicated time to spend with loved ones, we are able to foster open and honest communication, deepen our understanding of one another, and strengthen our emotional bonds. Quality time allows for meaningful conversations, where we can share our thoughts, feelings, and experiences in a safe and supportive environment.

Another important aspect of spending quality time together is the opportunity for mutual growth and personal development. When we engage in activities or conversations with others, we have the chance to learn from their perspectives, experiences, and knowledge. This shared learning can broaden our own horizons, challenge our beliefs, and promote personal growth. By spending quality time with others, we can gain new insights, expand our understanding of the world, and develop empathy and compassion for those around us.

Furthermore, spending quality time together provides a sense of comfort, support, and security in our relationships. When we make the effort to prioritize our relationships and invest in meaningful interactions, we are reassured of the love, care, and commitment that others have for us. Quality time can create a sense of closeness and intimacy, fostering a strong sense of connection and belonging within our relationships.

In addition to the emotional benefits, spending quality time together also promotes physical health and well-being. Engaging in shared activities, such as exercising, cooking, or exploring nature, can have positive effects on our physical health. Physical activities not only promote fitness and well-being but also stimulate the release of endorphins, which can improve our mood and reduce stress. By incorporating quality time into our routines, we can prioritize self-care, relaxation, and rejuvenation, leading to a healthier and more balanced lifestyle. Quality time allows us to connect on a deeper level, foster a sense of security and support, and promote physical health and well-being. As we navigate the complexities of our modern lives, it is important to remember the value of quality time and the positive impact it can have on our relationships and our lives as a whole.

# - Creating Meaningful Memories

Creating meaningful memories is a powerful way to enrich our lives and enhance our overall wellbeing. Memories are the building blocks of our identity and they shape our understanding of the world around us. Whether it's a cherished childhood memory, a special moment with a loved one, or a significant milestone in our lives, these memories hold a special place in our hearts and can bring us comfort and joy during difficult times. In this essay, we will explore the importance of creating meaningful memories, discuss strategies for making memories that last a lifetime, and offer insights on how to preserve and cherish these precious moments.

One of the key benefits of creating meaningful memories is that it can strengthen our emotional connections with others. Sharing experiences and creating new memories with family and friends can deepen our relationships and enhance our sense of belonging and community. Whether it's a family vacation, a holiday celebration, or a simple day spent together, these shared moments can create lasting bonds and bring us closer to the people we care about. Research has shown that positive memories can have a significant impact on our mental health and overall wellbeing, as they can boost our mood, reduce stress, and increase feelings of happiness and fulfillment.

In addition to strengthening relationships, meaningful memories can also provide us with a sense of purpose and direction in life. Reflecting on past experiences and celebrating significant milestones can help us define our values, set goals, and shape our future aspirations. By creating meaningful memories, we can establish a sense of continuity and coherence in our lives, as we connect our past, present, and future selves through shared experiences and cherished moments. This sense of continuity can help us navigate life's challenges and uncertainties with greater resilience and optimism, as we draw strength and inspiration from the positive memories we have created.

To make the most of our experiences and create meaningful memories that last a lifetime, it's important to be present and fully engage in the moment. Mindfulness and awareness are key to savoring the sights, sounds, and emotions of a particular experience, allowing us to fully appreciate its significance and value. By being mindful and present in the moment, we can enhance our ability to remember and cherish the details of a special experience, as well as the feelings and emotions associated with it. This can help us create vivid and lasting memories that we can revisit and cherish for years to come.

Another important aspect of creating meaningful memories is to prioritize experiences over material possessions. While material possessions can provide temporary satisfaction and pleasure, experiences have the power to create lasting memories that can enrich our lives in meaningful ways. Studies have shown that people tend to derive more happiness and fulfillment from experiences rather than material possessions, as experiences are more likely to foster social connections, personal growth, and emotional well-being. By investing in experiences that are meaningful and significant to us, we can create memories that have the power to shape our identity, values, and relationships in profound and lasting ways.

In order to preserve and cherish our meaningful memories, it's important to find ways to document and capture these moments in a tangible form. Whether it's through journaling, photography, scrapbooking, or other creative outlets, finding a way to record our memories can help us reflect on and relive these special moments in the future. Creating a memory book or a digital photo album can be a valuable way to organize and preserve our memories, allowing us to revisit and share these cherished moments with others. By taking the time to document and cherish our memories, we can ensure that they remain alive and vibrant in our hearts and minds for years to come. Memories have the power to shape our identity, strengthen our relationships, and provide us with a sense of purpose and direction. By being present, mindful, and intentional in our experiences, we can create lasting memories that have the power to bring us joy, comfort, and inspiration throughout our lives. By prioritizing experiences over material possessions, finding ways to document and preserve our memories, and sharing these cherished moments with others, we can cultivate a rich tapestry of memories that will sustain us and enrich our lives for years to come. Let us embrace the power of creating meaningful memories and cherish the moments that make our lives truly special.

# - Building a Supportive Network

Building a supportive network is essential for personal and professional growth. A supportive network is a group of individuals who offer encouragement, advice, and assistance when needed. This network can consist of friends, family members, colleagues, mentors, and other like-minded individuals. It is important to cultivate strong relationships within this network in order to thrive in both your personal and professional life.

One of the key benefits of having a supportive network is the emotional support it provides. Life can be challenging at times, and having a group of people who care about you and are there to listen can make a world of difference. Whether you are dealing with a difficult situation at work, going through a personal crisis, or simply feeling overwhelmed, having a support system in place can help you cope and navigate through difficult times.

In addition to emotional support, a supportive network can also provide valuable advice and guidance. When facing a tough decision or trying to achieve a particular goal, having access to different perspectives and insights can be invaluable. Your network can offer you advice based on their own experiences, suggest alternative solutions, and provide feedback on your ideas. This can help you make more informed decisions and avoid common pitfalls.

Furthermore, a supportive network can also offer practical assistance. Whether you need help with a project at work, advice on a personal matter, or simply someone to bounce ideas off of, your network can be there to lend a helping hand. By having a diverse group of individuals with different skills and expertise, you can tap into a wealth of knowledge and resources that can help you achieve your goals more efficiently.

Building a supportive network requires time and effort, but the benefits far outweigh the costs. One way to start building your network is by reaching out to your existing connections. This could include friends, family members, colleagues, classmates, or even acquaintances. Let them know that you value their support and would like to strengthen your relationship with them. By being open and proactive in your communication, you can lay the foundation for a strong and supportive network.

Another way to expand your network is by attending networking events, conferences, workshops, or other professional gatherings. These events provide a great opportunity to meet new people who share similar interests or goals. By engaging in conversations, exchanging contact information, and following up with individuals you meet, you can slowly expand your network and build meaningful relationships.

In addition, consider joining professional organizations, community groups, or online forums related to your field or interests. These platforms can connect you with like-minded individuals who can offer support, advice, and opportunities for collaboration. By actively participating in these groups, you can build credibility, establish yourself as a valuable member, and expand your network in a meaningful way.

It is important to remember that building a supportive network is a two-way street. Just as you seek support and assistance from your network, you should also be willing to offer your help and expertise to others. By being a supportive and reliable member of your network, you can strengthen your relationships, build trust, and create a sense of reciprocity that benefits everyone involved. By cultivating strong relationships with individuals who offer emotional support, advice, and practical assistance, you can navigate through challenges, make informed decisions, and achieve your goals more effectively. Remember to invest time and effort in nurturing your network, be open to new connections, and actively contribute to the success of others. By building a supportive network, you can create a strong foundation for success and fulfillment in all areas of your life.

# Chapter 19: Embracing the Rewards of Parenting

## - Celebrating Milestones and Achievements

Celebrating milestones and achievements is an important aspect of both personal and professional growth. These moments of success serve as a reinforcement of hard work and dedication, providing the individual with a sense of accomplishment and motivation to continue striving for greatness. Recognizing and celebrating milestones not only boosts morale and motivation but also helps to build a sense of community and camaraderie among colleagues. In the workplace, acknowledging achievements can foster a positive work environment and promote a culture of recognition, which ultimately leads to increased productivity and employee satisfaction.

One of the main reasons why celebrating milestones and achievements is crucial is that it helps individuals to reflect on their progress and see how far they have come. It allows them to pause and appreciate the hard work and effort that went into reaching a particular goal, which can be incredibly rewarding. By taking the time to recognize and celebrate milestones, individuals are able to build a sense of self-confidence and self-worth, knowing that their efforts have not gone unnoticed. This sense of validation can be a powerful motivator, pushing individuals to reach even higher goals in the future.

Furthermore, celebrating milestones and achievements can also have a positive impact on others around us. When we acknowledge the successes of our colleagues, friends, or family members, we show them that we value their hard work and dedication. This can foster a sense of teamwork and collaboration, as individuals feel supported and appreciated by their peers. Celebrating achievements together can also create a sense of unity and shared purpose, strengthening relationships and fostering a positive work or social environment.

In a professional setting, celebrating milestones and achievements is crucial for recognizing the contributions of employees and promoting a culture of continuous improvement. By acknowledging and celebrating the successes of individuals, organizations can showcase their commitment to recognizing hard work and dedication. This can help to boost employee morale, motivation, and engagement, leading to increased job satisfaction and higher levels of productivity. Additionally, celebrating achievements can help to create a positive work culture where individuals feel valued and appreciated for their efforts, leading to higher levels of retention and loyalty.

There are many ways to celebrate milestones and achievements, both in personal and professional settings. One common method is to host a celebration or recognition event, where individuals can come together to share their successes and stories. This can be a great way to build camaraderie and create a sense of community among colleagues. Another idea is to provide tangible rewards or incentives for reaching specific milestones, such as bonuses, promotions, or special recognition awards. These gestures can serve as a concrete symbol of achievement and provide individuals with a sense of pride and accomplishment. By taking the time to recognize and acknowledge our successes, we can build a sense of confidence, motivation, and pride in our accomplishments. Celebrating achievements not only benefits the individual but also fosters a positive work environment, promotes teamwork and collaboration, and showcases the value of hard work and dedication. It is important for individuals and organizations alike to celebrate milestones and achievements as a way to honor the effort and dedication that goes into reaching our goals.

## - Reflecting on Parenthood

Parenthood is a transformative journey that involves a myriad of emotions, challenges, and rewards. It is a role that requires immense dedication, selflessness, and unconditional love. As parents, we are tasked with nurturing, guiding, and providing for our children, while also instilling values and navigating the ups and downs of parenthood. Reflecting on parenthood allows us to contemplate the impact we have on our children's lives, as well as the ways in which they shape us as individuals.

One of the key aspects of parenthood is the profound sense of responsibility that comes with raising children. From the moment a child is born, parents are entrusted with the well-being and development of another human being. This responsibility can be daunting at times, as we strive to make the best decisions for our children and help them navigate the complexities of the world. Reflecting on this responsibility can bring about a sense of humility and gratitude for the opportunity to shape the future through our children.

Parenthood also brings with it a deep sense of love and connection that is unparalleled. The bond between parent and child is one of the strongest and most enduring relationships we will ever experience. This love is unconditional, unwavering, and transcends all boundaries. Reflecting on the love we have for our children allows us to appreciate the depth of our feelings and the joy that comes from nurturing and supporting them.

In addition to the joys of parenthood, there are also challenges that come with the role. Parenting requires patience, flexibility, and the ability to adapt to the ever-changing needs of our children. From sleepless nights with newborns to navigating the turbulent teenage years, parenthood is a journey filled with obstacles and hurdles. Reflecting on these challenges allows us to recognize our own strengths and weaknesses, as well as the importance of seeking support and guidance from others.

As parents, we also play a vital role in shaping our children's values, beliefs, and aspirations. We serve as role models, teachers, and guides, helping our children develop into compassionate, responsible, and resilient individuals. Reflecting on the impact we have on our children allows us to consider the values we are instilling in them and the legacy we are leaving for future generations.

Ultimately, reflecting on parenthood is a deeply personal and introspective process that can provide valuable insights into our own strengths and weaknesses, as well as our values and priorities. It allows us to appreciate the joys and challenges of parenting, while also recognizing the profound impact we have on our children's lives. By taking the time to reflect on parenthood, we can deepen our understanding of ourselves and our roles as parents, and strive to create a loving, nurturing, and supportive environment for our children to thrive.

# - Finding Joy in the Journey

As humans, we are constantly seeking happiness and joy in our lives. We often look for external sources of joy, such as material possessions, relationships, or achievements. However, true joy lies in the journey itself, not in the destination. It is important to find joy in the process of pursuing our goals, rather than solely focusing on the end result.

Finding joy in the journey requires a shift in mindset. Instead of fixating on the outcome, we should learn to appreciate the small victories and milestones along the way. Every step we take towards our goal is an achievement in itself, and we should celebrate these successes. By acknowledging and savoring each moment of progress, we can cultivate a sense of fulfillment and joy that sustains us throughout our journey.

One way to find joy in the journey is to practice gratitude. Gratitude allows us to focus on the positive aspects of our lives, no matter how small they may seem. By expressing gratitude for the opportunities and experiences that come our way, we can develop a sense of contentment and satisfaction that enhances our overall sense of joy. Gratitude shifts our perspective from what we lack to what we already have, helping us to find joy in the present moment.

Another key aspect of finding joy in the journey is to embrace challenges and setbacks as opportunities for growth. Life is full of ups and downs, and it is inevitable that we will encounter obstacles along the way. Rather than viewing challenges as roadblocks to our happiness, we should see them as opportunities for learning and development. Every setback is a chance to build resilience and strength, and overcoming challenges can be a source of immense joy and satisfaction.

Moreover, finding joy in the journey requires us to be fully present and mindful in each moment. Often, we get caught up in worrying about the future or dwelling on the past, which prevents us from fully experiencing the present moment. By practicing mindfulness and staying grounded in the here and now, we can appreciate the beauty and wonder of each moment as it unfolds. This mindfulness can deepen our sense of joy and fulfillment, as we learn to savor the richness of life's experiences.

In addition, finding joy in the journey involves cultivating a sense of purpose and meaning in our lives. When we have a clear sense of direction and alignment with our values, goals, and passions, we are more likely to find fulfillment and joy in our journey. By exploring our interests, pursuing our passions, and making a positive impact on the world around us, we can create a sense of purpose that fuels our journey with joy and enthusiasm.

Ultimately, finding joy in the journey is about embracing the process of growth, discovery, and exploration. It is about appreciating the moments of joy and fulfillment that come from pursuing our goals and aspirations, rather than waiting for a distant destination to bring us happiness. By shifting our mindset, practicing gratitude, embracing challenges, staying present, and cultivating a sense of purpose, we can find joy in every step of our journey. So, let us embark on this journey with curiosity, resilience, and an open heart, and may we find joy in the beauty and wonder of the path ahead.

# Chapter 20: Conclusion

## - Recap of Key Points

Recap of Key Points

In order to fully understand a topic, it is important to review and recap the key points that have been discussed. In this discussion, we will recap the key points that have been covered in relation to the topic at hand.

First and foremost, it is crucial to understand the main objectives and goals of the topic. By clearly defining the purpose of the topic, individuals can best understand what is being discussed and the importance of the information being presented. This sets the groundwork for further exploration and analysis of the topic.

Secondly, it is essential to consider the main points or arguments that have been made throughout the discussion. These points serve as the backbone of the topic and provide the framework for further examination. By identifying the main points, individuals can better grasp the core concepts being conveyed and can delve deeper into specific aspects of the topic.

Additionally, it is important to consider any supporting evidence or information that has been provided to bolster the main points. Supporting evidence can come in the form of research studies, data analysis, expert opinions, or real-world examples. This evidence helps to solidify the main points and provides further context for understanding the topic.

Furthermore, it is critical to consider any potential counterarguments or alternative viewpoints that may exist in relation to the topic. By acknowledging differing perspectives, individuals can gain a more comprehensive understanding of the subject matter and can engage in a more nuanced and balanced discussion. By clearly defining objectives, identifying main points, considering supporting evidence, and acknowledging alternative viewpoints, individuals can develop a more well-rounded comprehension of the topic at hand. This recap serves as a valuable tool for synthesizing information and forming informed opinions on the subject matter.

# - Final Thoughts on Great Parenting

Great parenting is a topic that has been studied and debated for decades, with experts offering a variety of opinions on what it means to be a successful and effective parent. As a parent myself, I have spent countless hours reading books, attending workshops, and seeking advice from trusted sources in an effort to become the best parent I can be. Through this journey, I have come to realize that great parenting is not about achieving perfection or following a set of rigid rules, but rather about cultivating a strong and loving relationship with your child based on mutual respect and understanding.

One of the most important aspects of great parenting is the ability to set boundaries and expectations for your child in a firm and consistent manner. Children thrive when they know what is expected of them and what the consequences will be if they fail to meet those expectations. This does not mean being authoritarian or punitive, but rather setting clear and reasonable guidelines that allow your child to develop a sense of responsibility and self-discipline.

In addition to setting boundaries, great parenting also involves providing a nurturing and supportive environment for your child to grow and thrive. This means being emotionally available and responsive to your child's needs, offering praise and encouragement for their accomplishments, and providing a safe and stable home environment where they can feel secure and loved. By creating a positive and supportive atmosphere, you can help your child build self-confidence, resilience, and a strong sense of self-worth.

Another key aspect of great parenting is fostering open and honest communication with your child. This means listening to their thoughts and feelings without judgment, being willing to discuss difficult topics in a calm and respectful manner, and being a good role model for effective communication skills. By fostering a strong and open line of communication with your child, you can help them develop strong interpersonal skills, problem-solving abilities, and emotional intelligence.

Great parenting also involves being actively involved in your child's life and taking an interest in their hobbies, interests, and passions. This means attending their school events, sports games, and performances, asking them about their day and listening attentively to their stories, and engaging in activities together that promote bonding and create lasting memories. By being present and engaged in your child's life, you can show them that you care about their well-being, value their unique qualities, and are committed to supporting their growth and development.

Ultimately, great parenting is about building a strong and loving relationship with your child based on trust, respect, and empathy. It is about being a consistent and reliable presence in their life, providing guidance and support when needed, and allowing them the freedom to explore and grow into the person they are meant to be. While no parent is perfect, by striving to be the best parent you can be and putting in the effort to cultivate a positive and nurturing relationship with your child, you can set them on a path to success and happiness that will last a lifetime. Remember, parenting is a journey, not a destination, and every moment you spend investing in your child's well-being is a moment well spent.

## - Continuing the Parenting Journey

Parenting is a journey that continues long after a child is born. It is a complex and challenging role that requires constant learning, adaptation, and growth. As children grow and develop, parents must also evolve in their parenting approach to meet the changing needs of their children. This journey may have its ups and downs, but it is ultimately a rewarding and fulfilling experience that shapes both the parent and the child.

One key aspect of continuing the parenting journey is understanding that each child is unique and may have different needs and personalities. What works for one child may not work for another, so it is important for parents to be flexible and open-minded in their approach. This requires parents to pay attention to their child's individual preferences, strengths, weaknesses, and interests, and tailor their parenting style accordingly. By recognizing and respecting the uniqueness of each child, parents can create a positive and nurturing environment that supports their child's growth and development.

Another important aspect of continuing the parenting journey is fostering a strong and positive relationship with your child. Communication is key in building a healthy parent-child bond, so parents should make an effort to listen to their child, validate their feelings, and engage in open and honest conversations. By fostering a strong relationship based on trust, respect, and communication, parents can create a supportive and loving environment that enables their child to thrive and develop into a confident and resilient individual.

It is also important for parents to set clear and consistent boundaries for their children. Boundaries provide structure and guidance for children, helping them understand what is expected of them and what behaviors are appropriate. Setting boundaries helps children develop self-discipline, responsibility, and respect for others. Parents should be firm but fair in enforcing boundaries and be consistent in their approach. By setting and enforcing clear boundaries, parents can help their children develop important life skills and values that will serve them well in the future.

As children grow older, parents must also adapt their parenting approach to meet the changing needs of their children. Adolescence can be a challenging time for both parents and children, as teenagers begin to assert their independence and develop their own identities. Parents may need to adjust their parenting style to give their teenager more autonomy and responsibility while still providing guidance and support. It is important for parents to strike a balance between giving their teenager freedom to make their own choices and setting limits to ensure their safety and well-being.

Continuing the parenting journey also involves taking care of yourself as a parent. Parenting can be demanding and stressful at times, and it is important for parents to prioritize self-care and well-being. Parents should make time for themselves to relax, recharge, and pursue their own interests and hobbies. This can help parents maintain their own physical and mental health, which in turn enables them to be more present and attentive parents to their children. Taking care of yourself as a parent is not only beneficial for your own well-being but also sets a positive example for your children on the importance of self-care and balance in life. By recognizing and respecting the uniqueness of each child, fostering a strong relationship with your child, setting clear boundaries, adapting your parenting approach to meet the changing needs of your children, and taking care of yourself as a parent, you can create a positive and nurturing environment that supports your child's growth and development. Parenting may have its challenges, but it is ultimately a rewarding and fulfilling experience that shapes both the parent and the child for a lifetime.

www.ingramcontent.com/pod-product-compliance
Lightning Source LLC
Chambersburg PA
CBHW072102150726
47999CB00005B/1838